THE INSANELY SIMPLE GUIDE TO THE SAMSUNG GALAXY Z FOLD 5 AND FLIP 5

UNLOCKING THE POWER OF THE LATEST SAMSUNG FOLDABLE PHONES

SCOTT LA COUNTE

RIDICULOUSLY
SIMPLE BOOKS

ANAHEIM, CALIFORNIA

www.RidiculouslySimpleBooks.com

Disclaimer: *Please note, while every effort has been made to ensure accuracy, this book is not endorsed by Samsung, Inc. and should be considered unofficial.*

Table of Contents

INTRODUCTION

Remember the old flip phones? Simple and small, with limited capabilities. They were soon replaced by smartphones that, while powerful, weren't as compact. But the tides are turning once more. Welcome to the era of foldable phones, a perfect blend of the past and the present.

The Samsung Fold5 isn't just a regular phone – it combines the nostalgia of the flip phone with the power and features of modern smartphones. If you're new to this fantastic foldable technology, this guide is your ticket to understanding and maximizing its potential. Let's see what you'll learn:

- How the Fold5 and Flip5 stands out in the world of iOS, Android, and other smartphones.
- Leveraging the perks of a folding screen.
- Getting familiar with the Stylus.
- Setting up your Fold5 for the first time.
- Making and receiving calls.
- Transforming your phone into a Desktop experience with Samsung DeX.
- Installing and managing apps.
- Capturing memories with the advanced camera.
- Browsing the Internet seamlessly.
- Using the Samsung SmartTag.
- Adjusting system settings to your preference.
- And so much more!

Ready to unfold the future? Dive into the guide and harness the full power of the Samsung Fold5 and Flip5.

NOTE: This guide is not endorsed by Samsung and should be considered unofficial.

[1]

GETTING TO KNOW YOU'RE YOUR SAMSUNG PHONE

This chapter will cover:
- What's new
- What's the difference between phones?
- Cosmetics of the phone
- How does it compare

WHAT A DIFFERENCE A PHONE MAKES

Every Samsung phone comes in lots of different configurations, but when buying a more high-end smartphone from Samsung, you are probably considering three: the S23, the Z Flip5, or the Z Fold5.

When it comes to foldable phones, you have two choices: the Fold5 and Flip5. Let's look at how they're different from earlier models and how they compare to the flagship Galaxy phone. But this year, Google also released a pretty stellar competitor: the Pixel Fold.

When you throw non-folding phones into the mix, then there's literally hundreds of options, but most readers will probably be asking one question: do I really want a foldable phone, or should I stick with an iPhone or S23?

So let's look at all the most popular phones and see how the Fold5—the high-end foldable phone—stacks up against the rest.

Samsung Fold5 vs. Samsung Fold4

To kick things off, let's stack the Fold5 up against last years model. Samsung hasn't taken a little bit of heat already for not making the Fold5 different enough from last year's model; there's truth to this, but there are differences.

To start off, the Fold5 is slightly smaller than the Fold4; this is big considering the phone is already…well, big! When it comes to putting your phone away, you'll have a thinner phone to manage.

The Fold5 is 253g (compared to 263g on the Fold4); you'll probably have a harder time noticing that. You'll also have a hard time noticing the difference in protective glass, but the Fold5 does use a newer version of Gorilla Glass that makes it even more durable—that's important when you consider the glass folds over and you could easily set something on top of it and scratch the screen.

The screen-to-body ration is better on the Fold5, but again, not by a lot (91.1% compared to 90.9% on the Fold4).

The Fold5 comes with Android 13 out of the box, but that's not a game-changer considering the Fold4 can easily upgrade to the newest version.

The camera hasn't changed a lot, but the Fold5 does support 8K at 30fps—the Fold4 only supported 8K at 24fps.

Wi-Fi on the Fold5 is tri-band as opposed to dual-band on the Fold4.

Finally the chipset (Snapdragon 8 Gen 2) and GPU (Adreno 740 GPU) on the Fold5 has been improved making the processing power faster and the graphics smoother.

Samsung Fold5 vs Pixel Fold

As I mentioned earlier, there's a new foldable in town and it's been all the buzz. It's the Google Fold—Google's first foray into the foldable marketplace. Does it live up to all the buzz when it compares to the Fold5? Let's find out.

When unfolded, the Pixel Fold has a slightly bigger screen (158.7x139.7x5.8 vs 154.9x129.9x6.1 on the Fold5); when using this as a work phone, that extra screen real estate goes a long way, but the tradeoff comes when you fold it. The Fold5 is a more narrow phone, which makes storing it a little easier.

While both phones have the same durable Gorilla Glass and water resistance, the Pixel Fold is a heavier phone (283g vs. 253g on the Fold5). So, again, when carry the phones around, the Fold5 will make a better travel companion.

Cameras are the bread and butter for most people when picking a phone; both these phones won't disappoint, but is one better? Both use a triple-camera setup (50MP wide, 10MP telephone, and 12MP ultrawide on the Fold5; 48MP wide, 10.9MP telephoto, and 10.9MP ultrawide for the Fold); the selfie camera on the Fold is better (8MP vs. 4MP on the Fold5). The differences are small, but where many will find Google has the edge is with AI enhancements; Google's software is known for improving the quality of phones through AI.

One edge, the Fold5 does have over the Pixel Fold is DeX support; DeX is enabled when you plug your phone into a monitor or screen—it essentially turns your phone into a working computer—it will feel very much like a cross between a Chromebook and Samsung UI. If you use your phone for work, you'll love this feature. And don't worry, it will be covered later in this book.

Samsung Fold5 and the iPhone 14 Pro Max

That comparison is great if you know for sure you want a folding phone. What if your still on the fence? How does the phone compare with the two biggest non-folding phones: the iPhone and S23?

Let's look first at the iPhone 14 Pro Max.

The Fold5 has more glass due to the folding nature, and having a front display, so it's not surprising that it's heavier—but not by much (253g vs. 140g on the iPhone 14 Pro Max)

They both have similar processors—though it's hard to compare sense iPhone uses its own hardware.

The Fold5 starts at a bigger size in terms of memory; it also offers more RAM (12GB vs 6GB on the iPhone Pro Max)

What about the camera setup? They're both pretty close—telephoto is slightly better, but not much. The iPhone does have a LiDAR scanner for depth sensing, which will become more important when their AR hardware is released.

So to sum it up, if you're ready for a foldable phone, it definitely stacks up against the highest end iPhone.

Samsung Fold5 and Samsung 23 Ultra

Last but not least, let's look at how the Fold5 compares next to Samsung's beloved high-end non-foldable smartphone: the S23 Ultra.

The S23 is unsurprisingly lighter (234g vs. 253g on the Fold5). The differences really start stopping there—both have a similar resolution on their screens; both have similar processors (though the S23 has less RAM: 8GB vs 12GB on the Fold5)

Things do get a bit of an upgrade when it comes to the camera setup on the S23; while they both have similar ultrawide and telephoto lenes, the S23 uses a quad lens setup with a wide lens that gets 200MP! Do you really need that much? That's a matter of debate, but if you're a photographer, the camera is definitely more impressive on the S23—not to say you'll be disappointed with the shots on the Fold5, however.

KEY Z FOLD5 FEATURES

The Galaxy Z Fold5 and Flip5, in many ways, is an S22 phone that happens to fold in two. If you can use the S23s, then you can use the Z Fold5 and Flip5. That means much of this book will be talking about features you will find on both devices. There are six key features that really shine on this phone:

1. Flex Mode - Flex mode enables when you fold your phone upward, then the app screen is divided in half on supported apps.
2. Multi-Window - The Flip lets you run two apps at once, showing them in split-screen. This is technically possible on non-foldable devices but works better on the Flip.
3. Large screen - Folded out, the device starts feeling more like a tablet than a phone.
4. Samsung DeX - If you want even larger, you can wirelessly use Samsung DeX, which brings your phone onto larger monitors. It essentially lets you use your phone like a computer when connected—so you can use things like a mouse and keyboard.
5. Camera - The cover screen window can also be used as a viewfinder when taking a selfie.
6. S Pen - The S Pen has been reconfigured just for foldable devices.

KEY Z FLIP5 FEATURES

The Galaxy Z Flip5, in many ways, is an S22 phone that happens to fold in two. If you can use the S22, then you can use the Z Flip5. That means much of this book will be talking about features you will find on both devices. Four key features makes the phone different:

1. Flex Mode - Flex mode enables when you fold your phone upward, then the app screen is divided in half on supported apps.
2. Multi-Window - The Flip lets you run two apps at once, showing them in split-screen. This is technically possible on non-foldable devices but works better on the Flip.

3. Cover screen - the small window on the front of the device has several widgets (such as weather and notifications) that show without unfolding the device.
4. Camera - The cover screen window can also be used as a viewfinder when taking a selfie.

HOW TO READ THIS BOOK

The idea of this book is to walk you through features in both the Flip5 and Fold5; but that also means some features won't work on your phone—especially if you have a Flip5, which doesn't have a lot of functionality of the Fold. If there's something you want to do referenced in this book and you can't, confirm that you are using the right device.

WHAT'S NEW IN ONE UI 5.1

Samsung's One UI is basically the look and feel they add to the Android system that powers their phones. Think of it as a unique dress that Android wears when it's on a Samsung phone. Over the years, Samsung has updated this "dress" in line with new Android versions.

Key Updates in Samsung One UI 5.1

- Expert RAW: For those who love taking photos, there's a new feature called Expert RAW. With one tap, this brings a professional camera mode for those who like to get creative with their shots.
- Improved Gallery: Samsung's photo gallery is now smarter! It can recognize faces in your photos and suggest sharing them with those friends. It can even identify objects within photos. Just press and hold on an item in a photo, and voila! It lets you save or share a cut-out of that object. Plus, want to know more about a picture? Swipe up, and you get all the details!
- New Widgets
- Battery Life: There are handy new widgets that show how much battery life your phone has, as well as any connected gadgets, like Samsung watches.

- Weather Updates: The weather widget now comes with cool animations to give you a feel of the day's weather.
- Personalized Modes: Imagine having different wallpapers for different times or activities, like a calm wallpaper for bedtime.
- Smart Routines: Routines are tasks your phone does automatically, like changing your ringtone or turning on airplane mode based on certain triggers. These have been expanded in the new update.
- Screenshot Sorting

[2]
THE SETUP

SETTING UP THE FOLD5

The first thing you need to realize about the Fold5 is it jumps between screens automatically; what I mean by that is if you are using the front screen and you want to unfold and go to the bigger screen, there's nothing you have to do--the screens change automatically.

This section is going to walk you through the setup. The setup is easy for a lot of people, so feel free to skip this section.

The first screen you'll see is the welcome screen. Most people will just tap the big blue Start; you can also use this screen to change the language (the default is English, but there's a drop-down to change it) or make an emergency call. You can also tap accessibility to access accessibility features (such as speaking the text that is on the screen).

If you are looking on the unfolded screen, then it will be narrow and more difficult to navigate.

Open it up and that same screen automatically appears on the bigger screen!

Next, you must check off that you agree to all the terms; tap Details next to each one if you really want to read them! Tap next when you have agreed to everything.

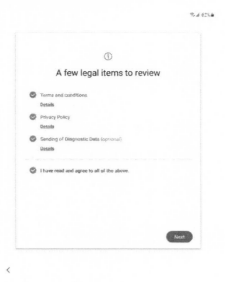

The next step lets you pick your wi-fi. This is optional, so you can tap next if you aren't near wi-fi. It is, however, recommended.

The next screen will just be a spinner that it's getting your phone ready. It will take a minute or two. If you need to get back to the previous screen now or in the future, you can also tap the arrow in the lower left corner.

If you have another phone, then the next screen will let you copy everything over. New to Samsung? That's fine! You can also copy from an Android or iPhone! It will guide you through the process. If you would rather set it up without doing this, then just tap Don't copy.

Once everything is copied (or you picked don't copy) you'll be asked to sign into your Google Account; don't have one? Use the Create Account button to make one for free. Or tap skip. I recommend getting one because A) it's free B) Google has a lot of free tools that will help you.

🤖 ⁴ 61%🔋

Google

Sign in

with your Google Account. Learn more

Email or phone

Forgot email?

Create account

Skip   Next

‹

Next you'll be asked if you want to turn on Back-up.

🤖 ⁴ 61%🔋

Google

Never lose your contacts

🔵 robescott@gmail.com

Have Google Contacts automatically sync device contacts so they're backed
up and available across Google services. They'll be on this device and
anywhere you sign in, including your next phone. Learn more

You can change this anytime in Google Contacts sync settings

Don't sync device contacts   Turn on Back up & sync

‹

If you select yes, you'll see even more delightful terms and conditions. Are you sick of those yet?!

After you agree to everything, it's time to decide how you want to unlock your phone: face recognition, fingerprints, pin, etc; it's advisable that you turn it on so if you ever lose your phone they can't access anything on it. But you can tap the skip button if you prefer not to. If you want to do facial recognition or fingerprint scanner, then you will still need to do a pin or pattern lock--these will be used as a backup.

🔒

Protect your phone

Prevent others from using this phone without your permission by activating device protection features.

Face recognition

Fingerprints

Pattern

PIN

Password

Skip

‹

Next, you'll need to sign into your Samsung account. If you don't have one you can get it free. Then you'll have to agree to more terms and conditions!

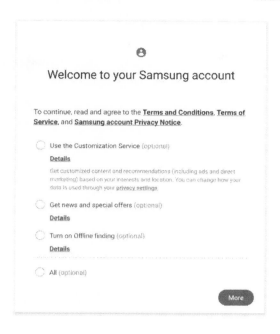

Finally you'll see a screen about how to care for your device, and then a finish button. Tap that and you are on your way to using the phone! Now the real fun begins!

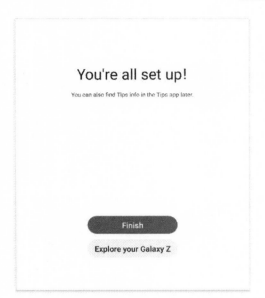

[3]

UNDERSTANDING THE USER INTERFACE

This chapter will cover:
- Exploring the Samsung UI
- Notification bar
- Edge bar
- Gestures

FINDING YOUR WAY AROUND

People come to the Samsung from all sorts of different places: iPhone, other Android phone, flip phone, two Styrofoam cups tied together with string. This next section is a crash course in the interface. If you've used Android before, then it might seem a little simple, so skip ahead if you already know all of this.

If any of this seems a little rushed, there's good reason: it is! We'll cover these points in more detail later. This is just a quick starter / reference.

When you see your main screen for the first time, you will see six components. They are (from top to bottom): the notification bar, add weather widget, Google Search app, short cuts icons, favorites bar, navigation.

Notifications bar - This is a pull down menu (slide down to expand it) and it's where you'll see all your alerts (new email or text, for example) and where you can go to change settings quickly.

Add weather widget – widgets are like mini apps that display information on your screen; weather is what's shown here, but they can be anything from Gmail, to calendars, and hundreds of things in between.

Google Search app – the Google Search app is another example of a widget. As the name implies, it can search Google for information; but it also searches apps on your phone.

Short cuts icons – these are apps that you frequently use and want quick access to.

Favorites bar – these are like short cuts, except you see them on all your screens. You can add whatever you want to this area, but these are the apps Samsung thinks you'll use most.

Navigation bar – These are shortcuts for getting around your phone; the first is the multi-task button, which helps you quickly switch apps; the next is the Home button which gets you back to the Home screen; and the last is the back button, which returns you to the previous screen.

So, what are these? Real quick, these are as follows:

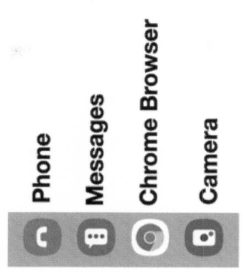

- **Phone**: Do you want to take a wild guess what the phone button does? If you said brings you an ice cream, then maybe you aren't cut out for a phone. But if you said something along the lines of "It launches an app to call people" then you'll have no problem at all with your new device. Surprise, surprise: this pricey gadget that plays games, takes pictures, and keeps you up to date on political ramblings on social media does one more interesting thing: it calls people!
- **Message**: Message might be a little more open-ended than "Phone"; that could mean email message, text messages, messages you keep getting on your bathroom mirror to put the toilet seat down. In this case, it means "text messages" (but really—put that toilet seat down...you aren't doing anyone any favors). This is the app you'll use whenever you want to text cute pictures of cats.
- **Chrome**: Whenever you want to surf the Internet, you'll use Chrome. There are actually several apps that do the same thing—like Firefox and Opera—but I recommend Chrome until you are comfortable with your phone. Personally, I think it's the best app for searching the Internet, but you'll soon learn that most things on the phone are about preference, and you may find another Internet browser that suits your needs more.
- **Camera**: This apps opens pictures of vintage cameras...just kidding! It's how you take pictures on your phone. You use this same app for videos as well.

NOTIFICATIONS BAR

Next to the short cut bar, the area you'll use the most is the notification bar. This is where you'll get, you guessed it, notifications! What's a notification? That's any kind of notice you have elected to receive. A few examples: text message alerts, email alerts, amber alerts, and apps that have updates.

When you drag your finger down from the notification bar, you'll get a list of several settings that you can adjust. Press and hold any of these options and you'll open an app with even more options.

From right to left these are the options you can change or use:

- Wi-fi
- Sound (tap to mute sounds)
- Bluetooth
- Lock the device from auto-rotating
- Airplane mode (which turns off wi-fi and Bluetooth)
- Flashlight

If you continue dragging down, this thin menu expands and there are a few more options.

The first is at the bottom of the screen—it's the slider, and it makes your device brighter or dimmer depending on which way you drag it.

Above that, there are several controls. Many of these controls are just an on / off toggle, but some let you long press to see expanded options. Some will be more obvious that others, but I'll go through each one quickly, starting from top left.

- Wi-Fi – Tap to turn off Wi-Fi; long press to change networks and see Wi-Fi settings.
- Sound – Tap to turn off sound; long press to see sound settings.
- Bluetooth – Turns off Bluetooth; long press to connect to a device or see Bluetooth settings.
- Autorotate – Tapping will lock the device orientation, so if you turn the device the screen will not rotate.
- Airplane mode – turns off features like Wi-Fi, cellular, and Bluetooth.
- Flashlight – Turns on the flash of your camera to let your phone act as a flashlight.
- Mobile Data – If you want to manually control if your phone is using mobile data or Wi-Fi, then you can toggle this on. There are a lot of reasons for this; sometimes you might find the Wi-Fi connection is too weak and you want to use mobile exclusively—but be careful: depending on what you are doing, mobile data can eat up your carriers data plan very quickly.
- Mobile hotspot – Toggling this on will let your phone act as a hotspot (so other devices can use your phone's Data connection to connect to the Internet); personally, I use this often to connect to my laptop on the go. Some carriers will charge extra for this service. You should also be

careful, as this does go into data charges; if you let someone else share it and they decide to stream a movie, it's going to eat up your data quick. Long pressing it will show you expanded settings.

- Power saving mode – turns on a power saving mode that will help your phone last longer; if you are low on batteries and not near a charger, this will help you get a little more life out of your phone. Long pressing it will bring up expanded power save features.
- Location – Toggling this on / off lets apps see your location; for example, if you are using a map for driving directions, it gives the app permission to see where you are located. Long pressing will show expanded location settings.
- Link to Windows – If you have a Windows computer, you can use this feature to send notifications to your linked Windows computer.
- Screen recorder – This option lets you create a video of what's on your screen; you can create a tutorial for something or even record a game. Long pressing will show expanded settings.

If you swipe you will see even more options to pick from.

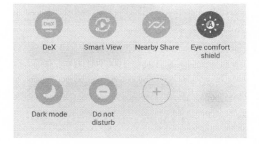

- DeX – DeX turns your phone into a desktop experience when connected to an HDMI monitor.
- Smart view – lets you mirror your screen (or sound) to other devices (such as a Google Home).
- Nearby Share – Let's you share photos and documents with phones nearby you.
- Eye comfort shield – Toggling on will turn off the blue light on your phone; it gives your phone a more brownish hue. Looking at a blue light can make it difficult to sleep, so it's recommended to turn this on at night.
- Do not disturb – Turns off notifications so you don't receive messages or phone calls (they'll go straight to voice mail); long pressing expands Do not disturb settings.
- Dark mode – Gives menus and some apps a black background instead of white. Long pressing will show expanded settings.

Samsung got rid of a lot of options that they probably felt either weren't used or weren't use that often. But they're still there. On the last notification screen, tap the + icon and you'll see more options that you can add.

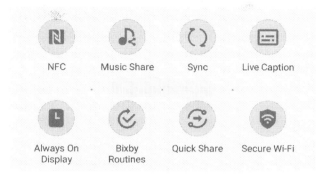

There are two screens of extra buttons (tap them and drag them to your notification bar to add them). The first screen shows:

- NFC – If you plan on putting credit cards on your phone to wirelessly pay for things at the checkout, make sure NFC is toggled on. Long pressing will show expanded settings.
- Music share – Shares music that you are listening to, so you can listen together. Long pressing will show expanded settings.
- Sync – Sync's your device across other devices.
- Live Captioning – This will be covered a little later, but toggling it on let's you add captions to your videos.
- Always on display – your display is always on when this is enabled. Long pressing will show expanded settings.
- Bixby routines – Sets up Bixby. Long pressing will show expanded settings.
- Quick share – This option lets you wirelessly share photos, videos and other files with another device. Long pressing will show expanded settings.
- Secure Wi-Fi – Creates a secure encryptions while using but public and personal wireless networks.

The next notification option screen has the following:

- Focus mode – Lets you set timers and turn off certain apps for a period of time to give you a more distraction-free experience. Long pressing will show expanded settings.
- Kids Home – Turns on kids mode, which gives your device a kid-friendly UI and turns off several apps.
- Enhanced Processioning – A mode that conserves battery by slowing your phone down.
- Wireless PowerShare – tapping this option lets you wirelessly power charge another wireless device (such as a watch or even another phone); your phone is essentially serving as a wireless charger to that other device. Long pressing it will bring up PowerShare settings.
- Call & text and other devices
- Secure folder – Creates a secure folder for your devices, so you can password protect certain apps and documents.
- Scan QR code – A QR code is sometimes seen on fliers; you can use this to scan it and see what the code links to.
- Dolby Amos – Toggling on will give your device superior Dolby Amos sound. Long pressing will show expanded settings.

On the notification area you'll also see two options for Media and Devices.

Media lets you control music and videos on other devices.

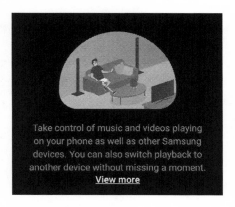

Devices lets you connect to devices using Bluetooth and see what devices you are already connected to.

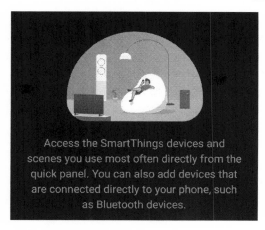

Access the SmartThings devices and scenes you use most often directly from the quick panel. You can also add devices that are connected directly to your phone, such as Bluetooth devices.

Up on top is a handful of other controls.

The config button brings up expanded settings for notifications.

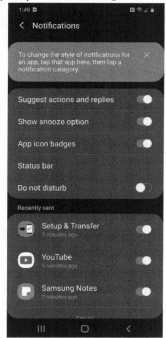

The power button will let you restart or power down your device.

GETTING AROUND QUICKLY

As mentioned, the bottom of the screen is your navigation area for getting around.

This is nice, but better is setting up gestures to handle navigating around your phone. This will turn this section off to give a tad more screen real estate.

To change it, swipe up from the bottom of your screen (this will bring up all your apps), then tap Settings. Next, go to the Display option.

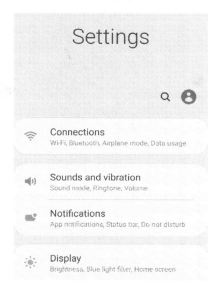

In Display options, scroll down until you get to Navigation bar, and then tap it.

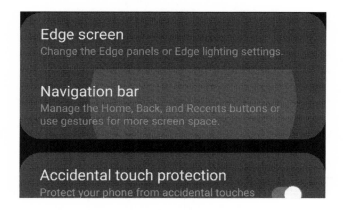

In the Navigation bar menu, select Full screen gestures.

Nice! It's gone! But what are the gestures?! Before you leave settings, it will give you a little preview of how they work, but below is a recap:

- Swipe up and release to get to your Home screen from any app.
- Swipe up and hold to bring up multitasking.
- Swipe right or left from the bottom edge of your screen to go backwards and forward.

You might recall that swiping up from the bottom showed you all your apps. That gesture now returns to the Home screen, so how do you see all your apps? From your Home screen, swipe up in the middle of the screen to see them.

When it comes to getting around your Samsung, learning how to use gestures will be the quickest, most effective method. You can change some of the gesture options by going to System > Gestures > System navigation.

The most important gesture is how to get back to the Home screen—there are no buttons after all. That's the easiest one to remember: swipe up from the bottom of the screen.

MULTITASKING

Those are the easy gestures to remember; if you want to move around quickly, however, you need to know the two big multitask gestures, which help you switch between apps.

The first is to see your open apps. To do this, swipe up like you're going to the Home screen, but keep going until about the middle of the screen and then stop and lift your finger—don't make a quick swipe-up gesture like you would when going Home. This will show you previews of all of your open apps, and you can swipe between them. Tap the one you want to open.

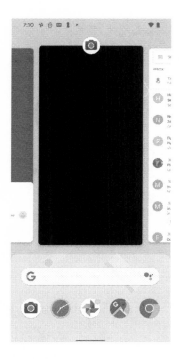

The quickest way to switch back and forth between two or three apps, however, is to swipe from left to right along the bottom edge of the screen. This swipes between apps in the order that you have used them.

ZOOM

Need to see text bigger? There are two ways to do that. Note: this works on many, but not all apps.

The first way is to pinch to zoom.

r with the Additic
: between you an
es. It is importan
Collectively, this l
s".

etween what the
al Terms say, ther
elation to that Se

The second way is to double tap on the text.

Rotate

You probably have noticed if you rotate your phone, it rotates the screen. What if you don't want to rotate the entire screen? You can turn that off very easily. Swipe down and then tap the "arrows" button to enable or disable it.

EDGE BAR

One of the features that has always stood out on Samsung devices is the way they make use of all areas of your phone…right up to the edge.

The Edge Bar brings up short cut menus quickly no matter where you are on the phone. To access it, swipe left from the side of your screen near the top; the edge bar outline can just barely be seen on your Home screen. It's right next to the down volume button and extends just above the up volume button.

Swiping right brings up a side menu.

On the bottom left corner, you can click the bulleted list icon to see all of your Edge Bar menus.

Swiping right and left lets you toggle between them.

Clicking on the config icon on the bottom left corner will let you select and deselect the Edge bar menus that are shown.

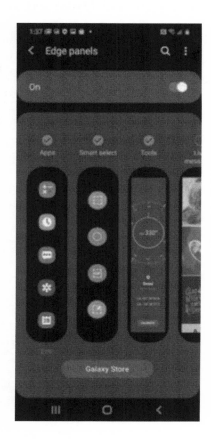

To add an app to the App Edge Bar menu, just tap the + icon.

To remove an app, tap and hold the icon, then drag it to remove. Smart Select is a tool to create screenshots and GIFs (little animated images).

Rectangle captures a selected rectangle area of your screen.

You can also go to somewhere like YouTube, where this tool would automatically located the video and record it to create a GIF. Use the GIF capture icon to do this.

The oval tool will change the capture into a circular shape.

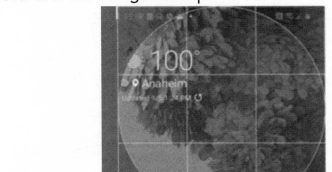

As the name implies, the Tools Edge Bar, has a series of tools that you can use along with your phone. They help you take measurements, keep tallies, use as a flashlight, or compass.

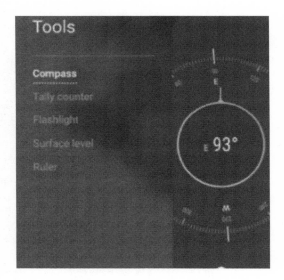

PIN THE EDGE BAR

There's a lot you can do with all the extra real estate; with all the extra space, one thing is pin the edge bar to the side so it's always there and you don't have to swipe to see it. This is an experimental feature, so to do it, you need to go to your Settings, then Advanced features, and finally click on Labs. On the Labs menu, switch the toggle next to Pin your favorite apps to on.

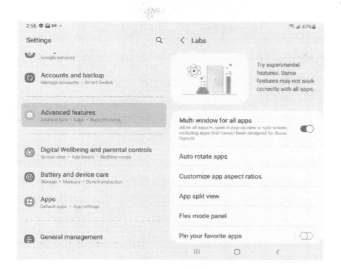

Previously, the edge bar would float on the screen like this.

When you Pin your favorite apps, it looks like the photo below.

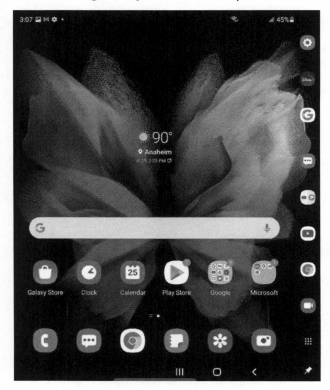

Now whenever you open an app, you will always see it off to the side--even if you rotate the screen.

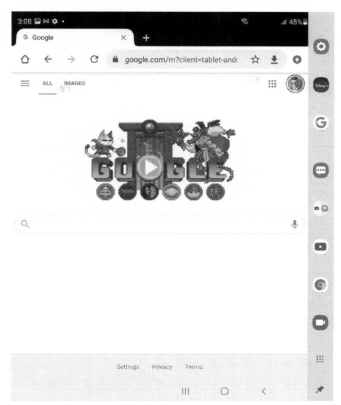

FLEX MODE PANEL

Flex Mode happens when you tilt your screen upward--it's ideal if you are using your phone like a tripod and half the screen is tilted up while the other half is flat.

Not all apps take advance of this mode, unfortunately; so some apps in this mode will look the same. Other apps, such as YouTube, will be optimized. YouTube in Flex Mode, for example, will show the video in the top half, and let you scroll through things like comments on the bottom half. The Camera app in Flex Mode, let's you see the viewfinder in the top half, while you scroll through pictures and set controls on the bottom.

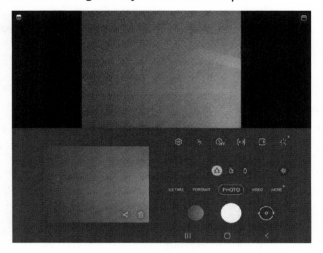

If you go to Settings, then Advanced features, and tap Flex mode panel, you can see a full list of supported apps. Some apps will also let you toggle the mode on and off--so, for example, if you don't want the app to work in this mode, you can just toggle it to off.

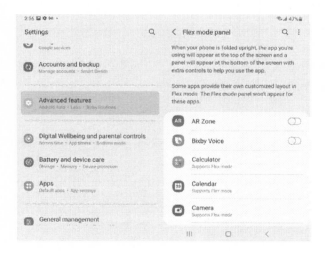

USING THE FLIP5 IN FLEX MODE

Flex Mode is easy to use: it's automatic. When the device is folded upright to a certain range, some apps will automatically change to take advantage of it. The camera, for example, will be a tripod mode where the top portion shows the viewfinder and the bottom half has the controls.

USING THE FLIP5 COVER SCREEN

The Cover Screen is very easy to use. If the Cover screen is off, press the side button or double-tap your screen to activate it.

If you get a notification, it will appear automatically (no need to tap); to view the notification, swipe right; to see more details, tap open app and unfold the phone—the app will launch automatically.

If you have music playing on your phone while it's folded, swipe left, and then the music controls will come right up—you can skip songs and pause the playback without opening your phone.

You can also change the brightness and sound by swiping down from the cover screen.

If a phone call comes in while the device is folded, it will show on the Cover Screen. You can answer or reject it without opening the phone. If the phone is not unfolded and you answer it, it will answer on Speakerphone.

If you want to change any of the settings here, go to Settings > Cover Screen. You can change the Clock Style from the settings, select the Widgets that show up on the Cover Screen, and turn on / off notifications that appear on the screen.

[4]

CUSTOMIZING THE PHONE

This chapter will cover:
- Customizing screens
- Split screens
- Gestures

MAKING PRETTY SCREENS

If you've used an iPhone or iPad, then you may notice the screen looks a little...bare. There are only a few buttons on it. Maybe you like that. If so, then good for you! Skip ahead. If you want to decorate that screen with shortcuts and widgets, then read on.

ADDING SHORTCUTS

Any app you want on this screen, just find it and then press and hold; when a menu comes up, drag it upward until the screen appears and move it to where you want it to go.

To remove an app from a screen, tap and hold, then tap Remove from the pop-up box.

WIDGETS

Shortcuts are nice, but widgets are better. Widgets are sort of like mini-programs that run on your screen. A common widget people put on their screen is the weather forecast. Throughout the day the widget will update automatically with up-to-date info.

It's such a popular widget that Samsung has put the option on your Home screen and you only have to tap it to set it up.

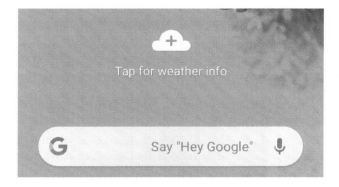

Once you add your city, it's going to automatically start showing. Clicking on it will open up the app.

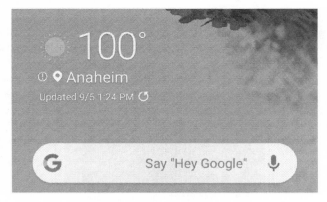

Weather is nice, but there are lots of widgets you can add to your Home screen. How do you get them?

There's actually a shortcut when you tap and hold over an app that has Widget capabilities (not all do).

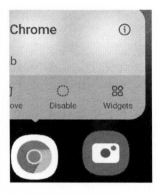

If you want to see all widgets available, then press and hold your finger on the middle of the screen. This brings up the Home screen options menu. Tap the Widgets icon.

This will show you the most popular widgets, but if you know what you want, then just search for it.

For this example, I searched for Gmail, who I know has a widget. I tap it, then it let's me select where I want it on the screen.

When you tap on the widget, you'll notice little dots on the side. That lets you make it bigger or smaller. Just drag it to your ideal width and height.

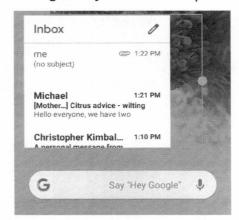

To remove any widget, just tap and hold it. From the pop-up, tap Remove from Home.

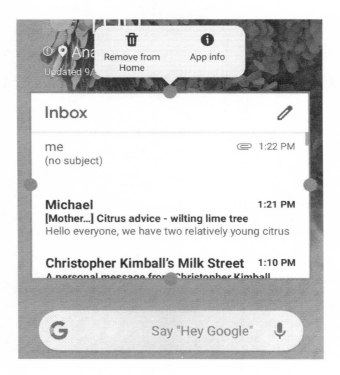

WALLPAPER

Adding wallpaper to your screen is done in a similar way. Tap and hold your finger on the Home screen, when the menu comes up, select "Wallpaper" instead of "Widgets."

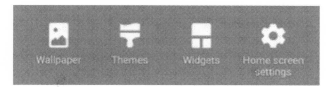

From the Wallpapers menu you have a few choices:
- My wallpapers – these are wallpapers you have purchased or ones that Samsung pre-loads
- Gallery – Pictures you've taken
- Explore more wallpapers – where you can buy wallpapers.

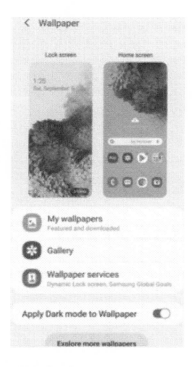

Buying wallpapers usually cost a buck. It's not an absurd amount of money, but you can also search for custom wallpapers on the Internet that are available for free.

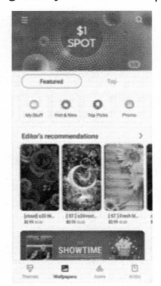

Samsung's featured wallpapers should not be overlooked. There's a lot to choose from.

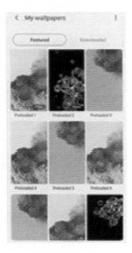

THEMES

Picking wallpaper for your phone helps give it a bit more personality, but themes helps really finetune the customization. You can pick icon shapes, fonts, and more.

To access it, press and hold on your Home screen, then select Themes.

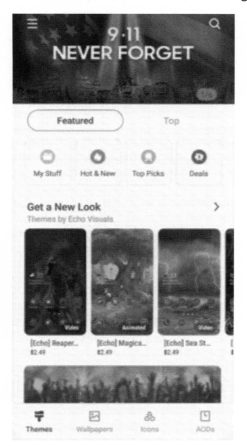

SAMSUNG DAILY

Samsung Daily is sort of like a recap of your day and daily recommendations for things to download. You can see it by swiping left from your Home screen.

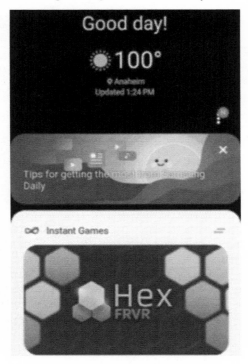

It's not the worst feature on the phone, but a lot of people don't really see value in it. If you rather not see it, then tap and hold on your Home screen, then swipe left when you see the Home options. On the Samsung Daily preview, toggle the switch to off.

ADDING SCREENS

Adding screens for even more shortcuts and widgets, is easy. Tap and hold the Home screen, and swipe to the right.

Next, click the + icon, which will add a screen. When you return to your home screen, you can swipe right and start adding shortcuts and widgets to it.

HOME SCREEN SETTINGS

To access even more Home screen settings, tap and hold the Home screen, then tap the config Home screen settings icon.

The first area that you'll probably want to change is the Home screen layout.

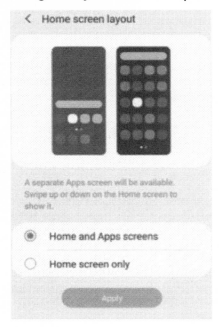

The home screen grid is also useful if you want to get a little more use out of the screen real estate; it adjust icon size / placement to fit more or less icons on the screen.

The rest of the settings are just toggle switches.

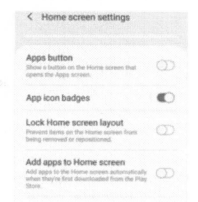

TWO CUSTOMIZATIONS IS BETTER THAN ONE!

The Z Fold has two screens (the outside one and inside one); by default they have the same wallpaper and similar feel. That doesn't have to be the case, however. You can have one set of icons and wallpaper / widgets on the outside.

And an entirely different look on the inside!

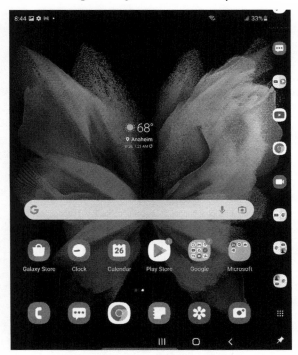

This can do wonders for productivity. Your outside screen is what you use the most casually. So you can have it arranged for easy access to things you might use without unfolding it—things like email and messages. Then on the inside screen, you can have the productivity apps that you use on the big display.

TOGGLING BETWEEN SCREENS

There are two screens on the Z Fold5: the Cover screen (folded mode) and the Main screen (unfolded mode).

What's brilliant about the way the Z Fold5 works is it's all seem less and automatic. If you are working on something one-handed on your cover screen, then fold it out, that same app appears, but it reconfigures to fit on the larger screen. Depending on the app, the layout will be completely changed on the larger device.

This isn't exactly true when you fold the screen back, unfortunately. By default, the app doesn't launch on that front display.

If you want to do that, then go to Settings, then tap display> Continue apps on cover screen—make sure that you have tapped the switch to continue the app on the cover screen.

From this menu, select the apps that you want to continue on the cover if you close the screen. If you don't select the app and you are using it on your large screen, then it will go in staby mode when you close it.

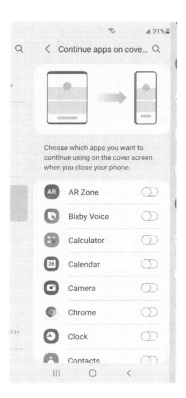

If you prefer to have the exact same layout on both screens, go to Settings > Home Screen > cover screen mirroring, and toggle it to On, then tap apply.

SCREEN MIRRORING

If you want your front and inside screen to be exactly the same (so the icons go in the exact same places), then you need to turn on Screen Mirroring. This is done on the Settings app; go to the home screen section, and tap Cover screen mirroring.

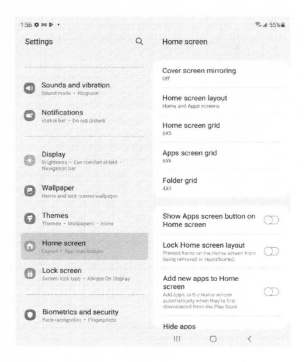

From here toggle off to on.

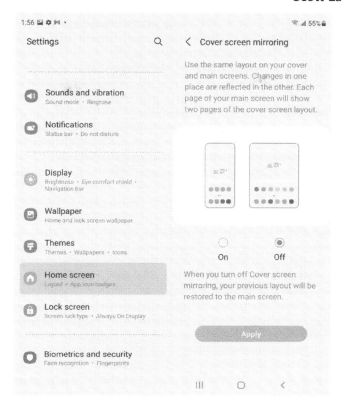

When you tap apply and return to your homescreen, you'll notice it's devices now into two screens.

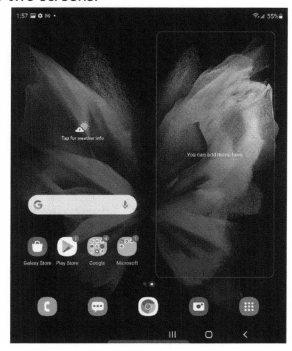

A WORD, OR TWO, ABOUT MENUS

It's pretty intuitive that if you tap on an icon, it opens the app. What's not so obvious is if you tap and hold there are other options. Every app is different. Usually, they're shortcuts—tapping and holding over the Phone icon, for example, brings up your favorites; doing the same thing over the camera brings up a selfie mode shortcut. Tap and hold over your favorite apps to see what shortcuts are available.

SPIT SCREENS

The Samsung phone comes in different sizes; the bigger screen obviously gives you a lot more space, which makes split screen apps a pretty handy feature. It works on the smaller Samsung as well, though it doesn't feel as effective on the smaller screen.

To use this feature, swipe up to bring up multitasking; next, tap the icon above the window you want to turn into split screen (note: this feature is not supported on all apps); if split screen is available, you'll see a menu that has an option for split screen.

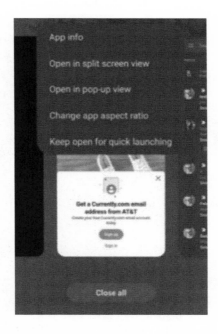

Once you tap "split screen," it will let you swipe left and right to find the app you want to split the screen with. Tap the one you want.

Your screen is now split in two.

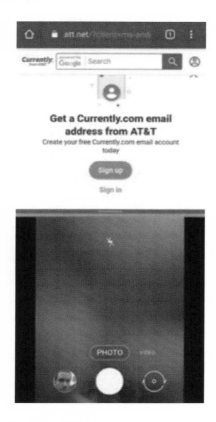

That thin blue bar in the middle is adjustable; you can move it up or down so one of the apps has more screen real estate.

To exit this mode, drag the black bar either all the way to the top or all the way to the bottom until one of the apps completely goes away.

With the large foldable phones, it make sense that you would want to do even more with split screen, so you can now have three apps on your screen at the same time.

To take advantage of that third split screen, open your Edge bar and drag the app you want to be in the third screen and drag it into the area of the screen you want it to be.

There's also a couple extra options in the middle of the screen—see those three little dots? When you tap that, you can rotate the windows or save them (so you can go back to that exact layout in the future).

GESTURES

Samsung has a few gestures built into the device that you can access by going into your settings app, then clicking Advanced features.

The first area to check out is Motions and gestures.

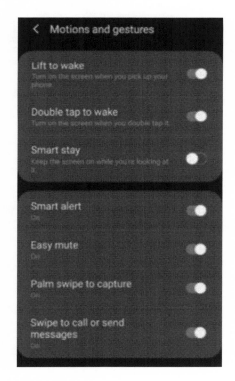

These are all toggle switches and you can see a preview of how they work by tapping on the title of the gesture.

The other setting is for One-handed mode. This turned off by default. By toggling it on, you can see the options available to you.

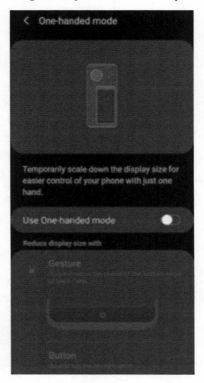

[5]
THE BASICS

Now that you have your phone set up and know your way around the device at its most basic level, let's go over the apps you'll be using the most that are currently on your shortcut or favorite bar:

- Phone
- Messages
- Chrome

Notice that Camera is off this list? There's a lot to cover with Camera, so I'll go over it in a separate chapter. In it's place, I will cover the Google Play store here, so you can begin downloading apps.

Before we get into it, there's something you need to know: how to open apps not on your favorite bar. It's easy. From your home screen, swipe up from the middle of the screen. Notice that menu that's appearing? That's where all the additional apps are.

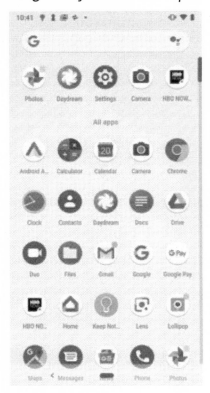

MAKING CALLS

So...who you going to call? Ghostbusters?!

You would be the most awesome person in the world if Ghostbusters was in your phone contacts! But before you can find that number in your contacts, it would probably help to know how to add a contact, find a contact, edit a contact, and put contacts into groups, right? So before we get to making calls, let's do baby steps and cover Contacts.

CONTACTS

So, let's open up the Contacts app to get started. See it? Not on your favorite bar, right? So where is it?! That's why I showed you earlier how to get to additional apps. Swipe up from the middle of your Home screen and keep swiping until the menu appears in its entirety.

It's in alphabetical order, so the Contacts app is in the C's. It looks like this:

Chances are if you've added your email account, you'll already have a lot of contacts listed. Like hundreds! There's going to be a message about merging them— that's up to you.

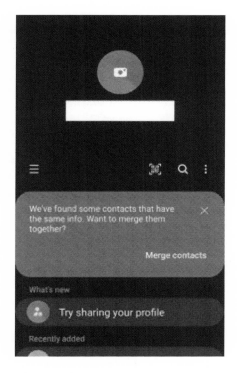

You can either search for the contact by clicking the magnifying glass, scroll slowly, or head to the right-hand side of the app and scroll—this lets you quickly scroll by letters. Just slide your finger until you see the letter of the contact you want and then stop.

I'm getting ahead of myself, however! Before you can scroll, it would be nice to know how to add a contact so there are people to scroll to. To add a contact, tap on that blue plus sign.

Before adding the contact, it will ask you where you want it saved—your Samsung account, the phone or Google. It's entirely up to you, but saving it to Google might save you some trouble if you switch to a different phone manufacture in the future.

Adding a person looks more like applying for a job than adding a contact. There are rows and rows of fields!

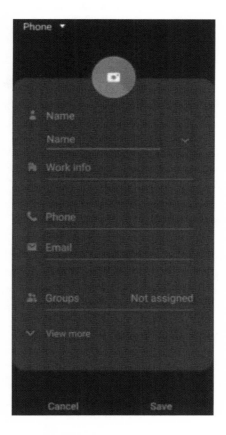

Just in case you weren't overwhelmed by all the fields, you can tap more fields and get even more!

Here's the most important thing you need to know: fields are optional! You can add a name and email and that's it. You don't even have to add their phone number. If you want to call them, then that would certainly help though.

If you have a hard time remembering who people are, then you can also take a picture or add a picture you already have. Comes in handy if you have eight kids and you can't remember if Joey is the one with blonde hair or red hair. Just tap the camera icon up top, then tap either Gallery (for assign a photo you've already taken) or Camera (to take a picture of them); you can also use one of the avatar type icons Samsung has.

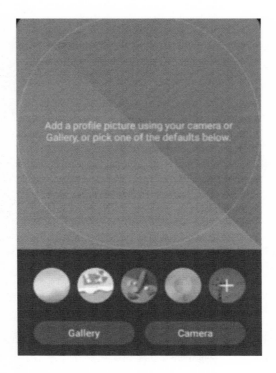

Once you are done, tap the save button.

EDITING A CONTACT

If you add an email and then later decide you should add a phone number, or if you want to edit anything else, then just find the name in your contacts and tap it once. This brings up all the info you've already added.

Go to the bottom of the screen and tap on the edit option button. This makes the contact editable. Go to your desired field and update. When you are finished make sure and tap Save.

SHARING A CONTACT

If you have your phone long enough, someone will ask you for so and so's phone number. The old-fashioned way was to write it down. But you have a smartphone, so you aren't old-fashioned!

The new way to share a number is to find the person in your contacts, tap their name, then tap Share on the bottom left corner of the screen.

From here you have a few options, but the easiest is to text or email the contact to your friend. This sends them a contact card. So if you have other information with that contact (such as email) then that will be sent over as well.

DELETE CONTACT

Deleting a contact is the same as sharing a contact. The only difference is once you tap their name, you tap the delete icon to the right (not the share to the left. This erases them from your phone, but not your life.

GET ORGANIZED

Once you start getting lots of contacts, then it's going to make finding someone more time-consuming. Groups helps. You can add a Group for "Family" for instance, and then stick all of your family members there.

When you open your contacts and tap those three lines in the upper left corner, you'll see a menu. This is where you'll see your Groups. So with Groups, you can jump right into that list and find the contact you need.

You can also send the entire group inside the Group an email or text message. So for instance, if your child is turning 2 and you want to remind everyone in your "Family" contact not to come, then just tap on that Group.

But what if you don't have labels? Or if you want to add people to a label? Easy. Remember that long application you used to add a contact? One of the fields was called "Groups." You have to tap more to see it. It's all the way at the bottom. One of the last fields, in fact.

If you've never added a label or want to add a new one, then just start typing. If you have another one that you'd like to use, then just tap the arrow and select it.

When you are done, don't forget to tap "Save."

You can also quickly assign to a group by tapping on the contacts name, then selecting Create Group from the upper right.

Once you tap that, you'll get to add a name, assign a ringtone, and assign other members.

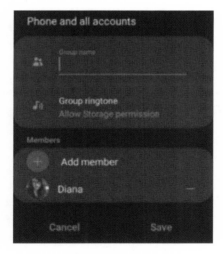

DELETE GROUP

If you decide you no longer want to have a label, then just go to the menu I showed you above—side menu, then the three dots. From here, tap the "Delete Group."

If there's just one person you want to boot from the label, then tap them and go to the Group and delete it.

MAKING CALLS

That concludes our sidetrack into the Contacts app. We can now return to getting back to making phone calls to the Ghostbusters.

You can make a call by opening the Contacts app, then selecting the contact, and then tapping on their phone number. Alternatively, you can tap on the Phone button from your Home screen or favorite bar.

There are a few options when you open this app. Let's talk about each one.

Starting from the far left is the Keypad tab. It's green because you are already there.

In the middle is the Recents tab. If you've made any calls, they'll show here.

The last option is Contacts, which opens a version of the Contacts app that's within the Phone app.

If you want to dial someone the old-fashioned way by tapping in numbers, then tap them, and tap the call icon. You can also tap the video icon to start a video call.

When you are done with the call, hit the "End" button on your phone.

ANSWER AND DECLINE CALLS

What do you do when someone calls you? Probably ignore it because it's a telemarketer!

It's easy to accept a call, however. When the phone rings, the number will appear and if the person is in your Contacts, then the name will appear as well. To answer, just swipe the "answer." To decline just drag the "decline."

PHONE SETTINGS

If you haven't noticed already, there's settings for pretty much everything. Samsung is a *highly* customizable phone. To get to settings, go to the upper right corner, then select Settings.

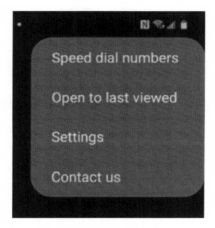

From settings you can set up ringtones, add numbers to block, set up your voicemail and much more.

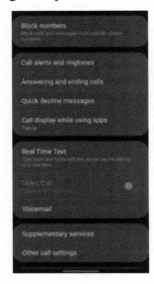

PLAY ANGRY BIRDS WHILE TALKING TO ANGRY MOM

What if you're on a call with your mom and she's just complaining about something, but you don't want to be rude and hang up? Easy. You multitask! This means you could play Angry Birds while talking!

To multitask, just swipe up from the bottom of your phone, and open the app you want to work in while you are talking. The call will show in the notification area. Tap it to return to the call.

MESSAGES

Now that you know how Contacts and Phone works, messaging will be like second nature. They share many of the same properties.

Let's open up the Messages app (it's on your Favorites bar).

CREATE / SEND A MESSAGE

When you have selected the contact(s) to send a message to, tap Compose. You can also manually type in the number in the text field.

You can add more than one contact--this is known as a group text.

The first time you send a message, it's going to probably look pretty bare like the image below. Assuming you have never sent one, it's going to be blank. Once you start getting messages, you can tap on "New category" to create a labels for them—so all your family messages, for example, will be in one place.

Once you are ready to send your first message, tap the message icon.

The top field is where you put who it's going to (or the group name if it's several people). You can use the + icon to find people in your contacts.

Use the text field to type out your message.

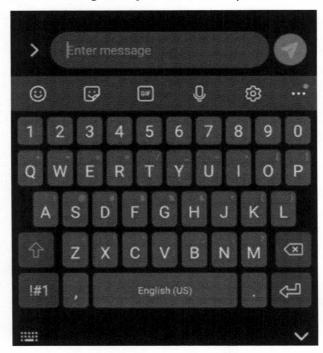

It looks pretty basic, but there's actually a *lot* here. Starting on the bottom, there's a little keyboard—that's to switch to a different type of keyboard; to the right of that is a down arrow, which will collapse the keyboard. To get it back, just click the message box again.

Just above the keyboard icon, is a "!#1" button, which will switch the alpha keyboard to a numeric / symbol keyboard (so you have quick access to symbols like @, ?, %)

Typing in another language or need an accent sign? Long press the letter and you'll reveal more characters and symbols for that letter.

Finally, at the top is a set of six additional icons.

From left to right, the first is the Emoji pack. If you want to respond to someone with an Emoji, then that's what you tap.

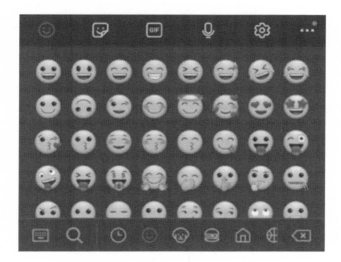

You can scroll through all of them, by swiping right, but because there's so many of them, they are also grouped together, and you can jump to a group by tapping on the associated image on the bottom.

Next to the Emoji icon is the Bitmoji sticker icon. I'll cover Bitmoji later, but for now, let's just say Bitmoji is like a emoji that is customized to look like you. To use it, you have to download it. It's free.

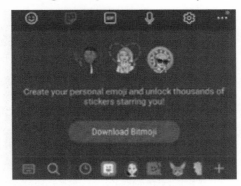

Next is the GIF search; you have to agree to the terms to use it. It's basically a search engine for GIF images; so if you want to find a birthday GIF to put in a message, for example, you could search "birthday" and see literally dozens and dozens of GIFs. If you don't know what a GIF is, they are small images that move on a loop—kind of like mini movies that last a couple seconds.

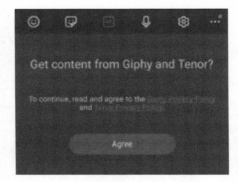

To the right of the GIF icon is the microphone icon, which let's you record a voice message instead of typing it.

You know Samsung loves it's settings, so it probably won't surprise you that the config icon launches keyboard settings.

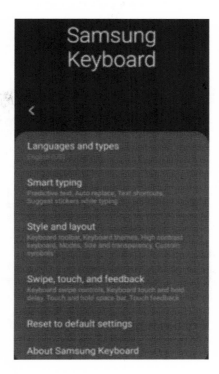

Because they love settings so much, there's a few more when you tap the three dots; you can adjust the keyboard size here, but also use some of the many other features—such as text editing and translation.

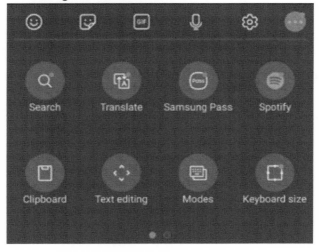

So, like I said, there's a lot to this keyboard. But the keyboard is only half the fun! Look above it…that little > icon will bring out some more things you can do with the message.

There are three additional options. The first is to include a picture that's in your photo gallery.

The next is to either take a photo or record a video.

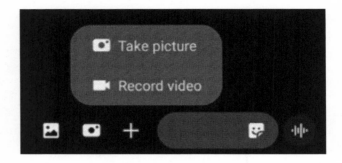

And the last is a series of extra options.

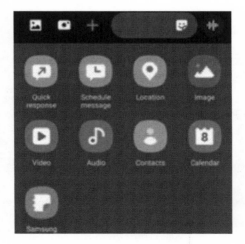

From left to right starting at the top:

- Quick response – gives a list of common responses so you don't have to type anything.
- Schedule message – let's you define when the message will be sent.
- Location – Shares where you are currently located with a person. So if a person is meeting you and they're saying "I'm looking for you, but don't see you!" you can send this to give them a better idea.
- Image / Video – this is similar to adding a video / image from your gallery (you can actually do that here as well), but it also searches for them in other places like Google Drive.

- Audio – share an audio file.
- Contacts – Share someone's contact information.
- Calendar – Share an event in your calendar with another person.
- Samsung – Share a Samsung Note with a person.

When you are ready to send your message, tap the arrow with the SMS under it.

VIEW MESSAGE

When you get a message, your phone will vibrate, chirp, or do nothing—it all depends on how you set up your phone. To view the message, you can either open the app, or swipe down to see your notifications—one will be the text message.

WHERE'S AN APP FOR THAT?

I mentioned earlier that you could play Angry Birds while talking to your angry mom on the phone. Sound fun? But where is Angry Birds on your phone? It's not! You have to download it.

Adding and removing apps on the Galaxy is easy. Head to your favorite bar on the bottom of your Home screen and tap the Google Play app.

This launches the Play Store.

From here you can browse the top apps, see editors' picks, look through categories, or, if you have an app in mind, search for it. The Play Store isn't just for apps. You can use the tabs on the top to go to movies, books, and music. Any kind of downloadable content that's offered by Google can be found here.

When you see the app you want, tap on it. You can read through reviews, see screenshots, and install it on your phone. To install, simply tap the install button—if it's a paid app you'll be prompted to buy it. If there's no price, it's free (or offers in-app payments—which means the app is free, but there are premium features inside it you may have to pay for).

The app is now stored in the app section of your device (remember the section you get to when you swipe up from the bottom to the top?).

REMOVE APP

If you decide you no longer want an app, go to the app in the app menu and tap and hold it. This brings up a box with a few options. The one you want is Uninstall.

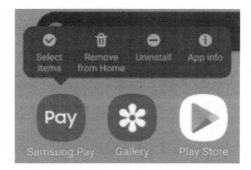

If you download the app from the Play Store, you can always delete it. Some apps that were pre-installed on your phone cannot be deleted.

DRIVING DIRECTIONS

Back in the day, you may have had a GPS. It was a fancy plastic device that would give you directions for anywhere in North America. You can throw out that device because your phone is your new GPS.

To get directions, swipe up to open up your apps, and go to the Google folder. Tap the Maps app.

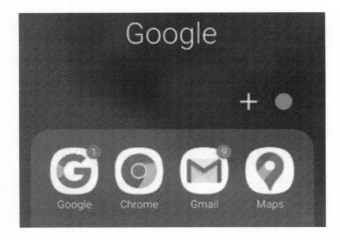

It's automatically going to be set to wherever you are currently at—which is both creepy and useful.

To get started, just type where you want to go. I'm searching for Disneyland, Anaheim.

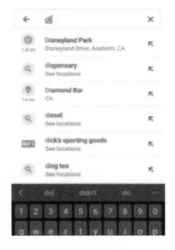

It automatically starts filling in what it thinks you are going to type and tells you the distance. When you see the one you want, tap it.

It pinpoints the location on the map and also gives you an option to call, share or get directions to the location. If you want to zoom out or in, just use two fingers and pinch in or out on the screen.

It automatically gets directions from where you are. Want it from a different location? Just tap on the "Your location" field and type where you want to go. You can also reverse the directions by tapping on the double arrows. When you are ready to go, tap "Start."

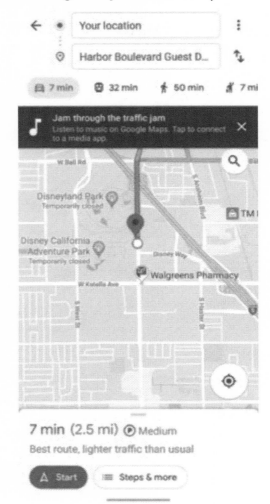

What if you don't want to drive? What if you want to walk? Or bike? Or take a taxi? There are options for all of those and more! Tap the slider under the address bar to whatever you prefer. This updates the directions—when you walk, for example, it will show you one-way streets and also update the time it will take you.

What if you want to drive but are like me: terrified of freeways in California? There's an option to avoid highways. Tap the menu button in the upper right corner of the screen, and select Route options (there's actually lots of other things packed in here like adding stops, sharing directions, and sharing your location).

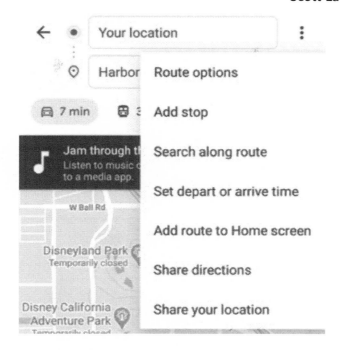

In the Route options, select what you want to avoid, and hit "done." You are now rerouted to a longer route—notice how the times probably changed?

Once you get your directions, you can swipe up to get turn-by-turn directions.

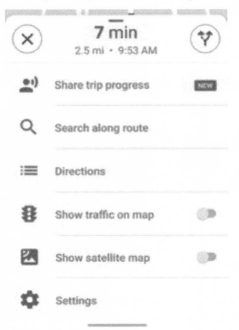

You can even see what it looks like from the street. It's called Street View.

Street View isn't only for streets. Google is expanding the feature everywhere. If you hold your finger over the map, there will be an option to show Street View if it's available. Just tap the thumbnail. Here's a Street View of Disneyland:

You can wander around the entire park! If only you could ride the rides, too! You can get even closer to the action by picking up the Dreamview headset. When you stick your phone in that, you can turn your head and the view turns with you.

Street View is also available in a lot of malls and other tourist attractions. Point your map to the Smithsonian in Washington, DC and get a pretty cool Street View.

LIVE CAPTIONING

One of the bigger features to Android 10 is live captioning; live captioning can transcribe any video you record and show what's being said. It works surprisingly well and is pretty accurate.

To turn it on, go to Settings > Accessibility > Hearing enhancements > Live caption.

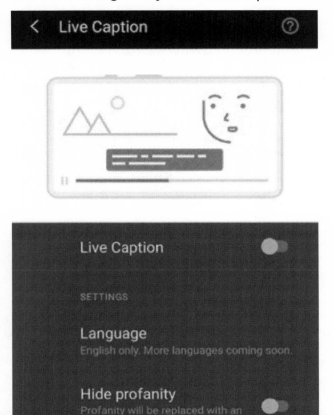

In the settings, you can also toggle off profanity, and, coming soon, select a different language. If it's something you'd only occasionally use, I recommend leaving it toggled off, but having it toggle on under Live Caption in volume control. With that toggled on, all you have to do is press the volume button. Once you do that, you'll see the option to turn it on; it's the bottom option.

Once it's on, you'll start seeing a transcription appear in seconds.

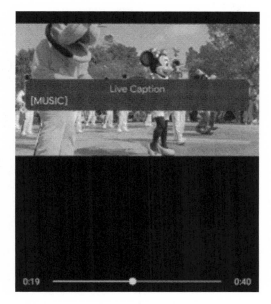

REFRESH RATE

The Galaxy supports up to 120Hz refresh rate. Wow, right? Actually, most people have no idea what this means. It's frames per second (FPS)—or 120 FPS. So, what does that mean? If you're playing games or using something that has fast moving action, it means things will seem a lot smoother. It will also eat your battery life to shreds, so use with caution (60Hz is the norm).

To toggle it on go to Settings > Display > Motion smoothness.

Next, select 120 Hz.

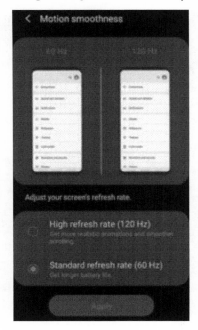

I recommend turning it on just to see what it looks like, but if you are not just absolutely blow away by it, then turn it off so you can have a longer lasting battery.

SHARING WI-FI

Anytime you have guests over, you almost always get the question: what's your wi-fi password. If you are like me, then it probably annoys you. Maybe your password is really long, maybe you just don't like giving out your password, or maybe you are just too embarrassed to say that it's "Feet$FetishLover1." Whatever the reason, then you will love sharing your wi-fi with QR codes. Gone are the days of giving this info out. Just give them a code that they scan, and they'll have access without ever knowing what your password is.

To use it, go to your wi-fi settings, then select the Wi-Fi options and Wi-Fi Direct.

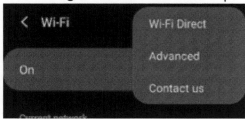

Make sure both devices have Wi-Fi on and follow the directioons.

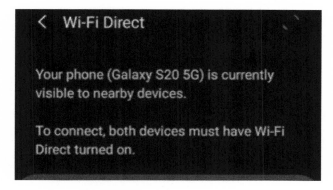

SAMSUNG KIDS

One place Samsung truly shines above other companies is with its parental control features and kids mode. Yes, other devices have parental controls, but Samsung takes it up a nauch by creating a UI that's just for kids.

With kids mode, you can quickly toggle it on and off for those moments where you need to distract a child.

To access it, swipe down to bring down your notification bar, then swipe right one time. You'll see it in the second row. Tap it.

The first time you launch it, you'll have to download a very small program. It will take a few seconds depending on your connection speed.

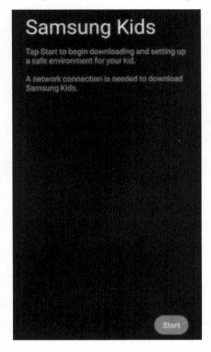

Once it's done downloading, you'll see the welcome screen, and be asked if you want to create a shortcut on your desktop. Tap start when you are ready.

Once you tap next, you'll get to the main Samsung Kids UI. It looks a little like your phone…only cuter! There's a handful of icons on the screen, but you'll notice they each have download buttons. That's because they aren't installed yet. You have to tap the download button for each app you want to install (not more than three at a time.

Swipe to your left, and you'll see non-Samsung apps. These need to be downloaded as well.

You might be thinking, how safe can this mode be? There's an Internet browser right on the Home screen! Tap it and let's see!

You'll notice right away that this is not yo mama's Internet! The only websites they can access are the ones you add. Want to add one? Tap the +New website button.

You'll quickly notice that all the apps in this mode are very stripped down. Even the camera app, which is pretty harmless, has few features. There's a shutter, a toggle for photos and videos, and a button for effects.

The phone is the same way. Your child can't open the app and call anyone. They can only call numbers that you've added. Want to add someone? Just tap the + icon.

The pre-installed apps are all pretty harmless, and borderline educational.

If there's apps you want to remove or install, then tap the option button in the upper right corner.

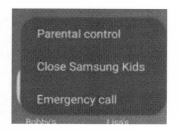

Once you put in your pin, you'll have access to the settings. Here you'll be able to control what your child does and how long they do it for. You can also monitor what they've been doing. You can control how much they can spend on something like games and something like reading.

Is there a pre-installed app that you don't want your child to see? No problem! Scroll down a little, and tap the Apps option.

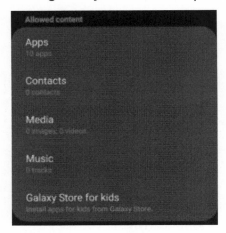

From the options button, select remove and then select the app that you want removed.

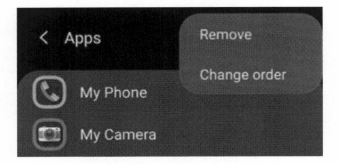

What app other apps? Like third part ones? Return to that list and select Galaxy Store for kids. That's going to take you to a custom kids store. It's not going to have teen or adult games—it's only games that are appropriate for kids.

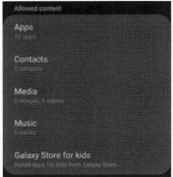

Tap the download option next to any app that you want to download. They'll show up when you swipe right from kids Home screen.

So that's all well and good, but what happens when you want to return to adulthood? How do you get out of this mode? It takes just a second! On the home screen, tap the back icon. It will ask you for your pin code. Once you add it, you are back in normal mode. That's it!

SAMSUNG DEX MODE

Samsung DeX Mode is one of the most underrated features of the high-end Samsung phone and tablet models. It's not available on cheaper models (such as the Flip5, unfortunately).

What is it? DeX stands for Desktop Experience, which should give you a hint of what the mode does; in a nutshell: it turns your mobile phone or tablet into an actual computer.

If you've ever used CarPlay or Android Auto in your car, then you might have an idea of what that means; plug in your phone or tablet into a monitor and everything is resized for the larger screen; connect a mouse and keyboard and suddenly you have a real computer-like experience. The below image is the Fold5 in DeX mode.

If you've used a Chromebook, then this mode will probably look familiar to you because many Chromebook features exists in it.

To use it, you obviously need a monitor; Samsung used to support a MacOS and Windows OS app; you probably can still find a copy of the app, but not being supported by Samsung anymore will probably mean you experiences bugs—or it doesn't work at all.

My suggestion, if you want to use your phone as a desktop computer, is to invest in something called a Side Monitor or Portable Monitor; these monitors are typically used as slim companions to a laptop; because they're secondary screens, the resolution isn't as sharp, but you can also get them at a reasonable price—online retailers frequently sell them for $150 to $200. You do want to doublecheck that it comes with a HDMI to USB-C cable to plug into your phone; you'll also need to make sure it includes a power adapter for the monitor itself.

DeX mode is a plug and play interface, which means as soon as you plug the monitor into the phone, everything is seamless—you don't have to press anything or launch an app.

To take full advantage of the mode, you want a Bluetooth keyboard and a mouse. If you want to save a little bit of money, however, you can use the phone itself as a mouse.

To do this, when your phone is plugged into the monitor and DeX mode is showing on the screen, tap the monitor icon on the lower left side of your phone.

This turns your phone into a large trackpad. Double tap to exit the mouse mode.

Because newer Android apps are usually built to support both a mobile and desktop environment, you should notice most apps will take full advantage of the extra screen real estate. As an example, here's Microsoft Word as it appears on the Fold5.

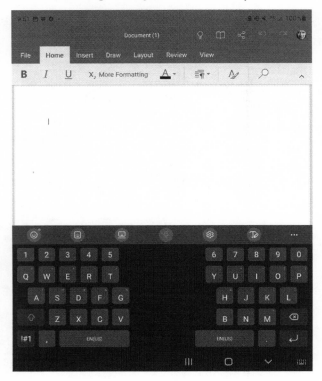

Plug it into a monitor and start DeX mode, and Microsoft Word looks like this.

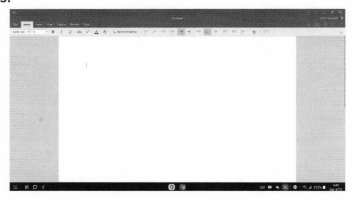

Here's PowerPoint in DeX mode.

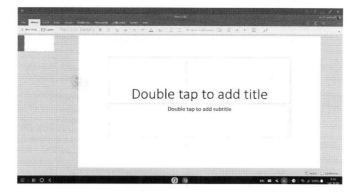

And here's Excel.

That extra screen real estate is pretty nice, isn't it?!

Using DeX is not really any different than using your phone. So once you have a handle of how your phone works, you'll have no problem navigating around DeX.

SMARTTAGS

If you bought your Galaxy phone when it was first released, then chances are it was bundled with a SmartTag; if not, it is $29.99.

SmartTag is an optional accessory for finding your gadgets and devices. You can attach it to your king ring, stick it on a remote, put it in your purse, or wherever you might lose something. If you can't find your keys, then from your phone you can ping it and the SmartTag will start ringing.

You can also connect your SmartTag to smart home devices like lights and doors; so when you come up, you can double click your tag to perform an action—like turn on the lights.

SmartTag connects to your phone with Bluetooth and runs on a battery. As long as you aren't pinging your device every five minutes, you shouldn't have to replace the battery very often.

To get started, go to the SmartThings app from the Samsung folder of all apps; if you don't have it, you can download it free from the app store. It's included with the newest OS update, so chances are it's there if you have a new phone.

The first time the app opens, you'll have to agree to the terms and conditions.

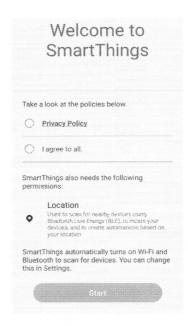

Once you click start, press the button on the tag and it should find it right away. Make sure and tap "While using the app" on the next screen.

If the tag will always be in a particular room, then you can name it; otherwise just skip it.

Next it will ask if you want to add the device now or later. Tap Add Now.

Next, confirm that the tag can know your location. It needs to know the location to properly work.

Click start next.

It will take a few seconds to set everything up.

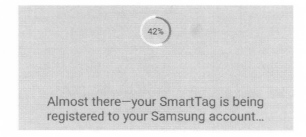

When it's done, you'll be prompted to name the tag. You can keep it as SmartTag, but being more descriptive (i.e. calling it car keys) is advisable if you have several SmartTag's.

You'll see a couple of setup screens, then it will ask you if you want to update the SmartTag; I recommend doing this. It is very quick and it makes sure the SmartTag is free of any bugs.

Once it's done, you'll see your main screen; click Get Started.

Next, download the add-on software.

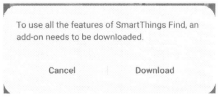

Once you're finished, you can open the software again and you'll be able to tap the music icon to ping your SmartTag; when you do, it will start to ring.

[6]

SURFING THE INTERNET

When it comes to the Internet, there are two things you'll want to do:
- Send email
- Browse the Internet

ADD AN EMAIL ACCOUNT

When you set up your phone, you'll set it up to your Google Account, which is usually your email.

You may, however, want to add another email account—or remove the one you set up.

To add an email, swipe up to bring up your apps, and tap on "Settings."

Next, tap on "Accounts."

From here, select "Add Account"; you can also tap on the account that's been set up and tap remove account—but remember you can have more than one account on your phone.

Once you add your email, you'll be asked what type of email it is. Follow the steps after you select the email type to add in your email, password, and other required fields.

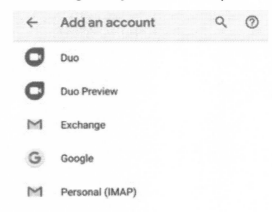

CREATE AND SEND AN EMAIL

To send an email using Gmail (Samsung's native email app), swipe up to get to your apps, tap "Gmail," and tap "Compose a New Email" (the little round red pencil in the lower right corner). When you're done, tap the send button.

You can also use the Google Play Store to find other email apps (such as Outlook).

MANAGE MULTIPLE EMAIL ACCOUNTS

If you have more than one Gmail account, tap the three lines at the upper left of your email screen; this brings out a slider menu. If you tap on the little arrow next to the email address, it drops down and will show other accounts. If none are listed, you can add one.

SURFING THE INTERNET

Google's native Web browser is Chrome. You can use other browsers (which can be found in the Google Play Store). This book will only cover Chrome, however.

Get started by tapping on the Chrome browser icon from your favorite bar, or by going into all programs.

If you've used Chrome on a desktop or any other device, then this chapter won't exactly be rocket science—just like the email app, many of the same properties you find on the desktop exist on the mobile version.

When you open it, you'll see it's a pretty basic browser. There are three main things that you'll want to note.

- **Address Bar** - As you would guess, this is where you put the Internet address you want to go to (google.com, for example); what you should understand, however is that this is not just an address bar. This is a search bar. You can use it to search for things just as you would searching for something on Google; when you hit the enter key, it takes you to the Google search results page.

- **Tab Button** - Because you are limited in space, you don't actually see all your tabs like you would on a normal browser; instead you get a button that tells you how many tabs are open. If you tap it, you can either toggle between the tabs, or swipe over one of the pages to close the tab.

- **Menu Button** - The last button brings up a menu with a series of other options that I'll talk about next.

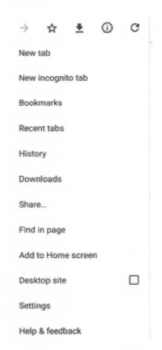

The menu is pretty straightforward, but there are a few things worth noting.

"New incognito tab" opens your phone into private browsing; that doesn't mean your IP isn't tracked. It means your history isn't record; it also means passwords and cookies aren't stored.

A little bit further down is "History"; if you want your history erased so there's no record on your phone of where you went, then go here, and clear your browsing history.

If you want to erase more than just websites (passwords, for example) then go to "Settings" at the very bottom of the menu. This opens up more advance settings.

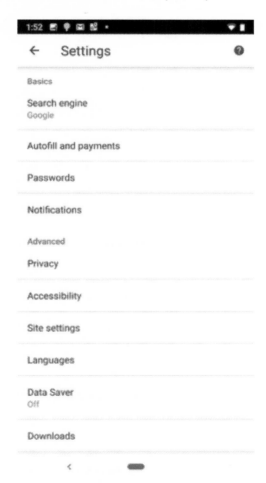

[7]

UNDERSTANDING THE CAMERA

The camera is the bread and butter of the Samsung phone. Many people consider the Samsung Galaxy to be the greatest camera ever on a phone. I'll leave that for you to decide. Personally, I think all top tier phone cameras have their own pros and cons.

This chapter is based off the Galaxy Ultra. As mentioned earlier in the book, not all smartphones are alike in terms of cameras; it's one of the most noticeable differences with the phones. The Ultra has more lens, more zoom and more pixels.

This means that if you are using a non-Ultra phone, some of the things mentioned in this chapter won't apply to you. So if you are reading and thinking "where is that on my phone" then you probably don't have an Ultra.

THE BASICS

Are you ready to get your Ansel Adams on? Let's get started by opening the Camera app

When you open the app, it starts in the basic camera mode. The UI can look pretty simple, but don't be fooled. There are a lot of controls.

On the bottom of the screen is the shutter (to take your photo)—swipe it down to take a "burst shot" which takes several photos at once, and hold it down to toggle to video. To the right of the shutter is the camera flip—to switch to the front camera.

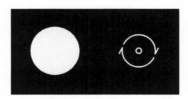

Up on the top of the camera app is where you'll find the majority of your settings.

Starting from left to right, there is the settings icon. Most of the settings are just toggle switches and easy to understand.

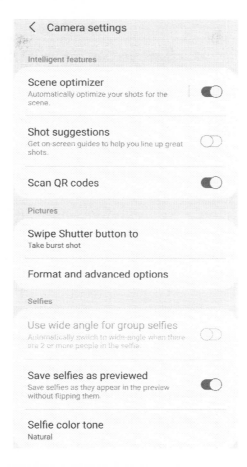

Next to that is the flash setting. Tapping that will let you select no flash, auto flash, or force flash.

The next option is the timer. This lets you delay when the photo will be taken. It's best used with a tripod.

The next option lets you pick how large the photo will be. The best option is 108 MB. That's going to give you an unbelievably *huge* image. It's also going to take away the next two options. If you notice they're grayed out…that's why. This is the only mode that you cannot use them on.

And what are those two options? The first toggles Motion on and off. And the second lets you use special filters to enhance the photo.

One final note on photos (and this applies to videos as well): to zoom, you pinch in and out.

CAMERA MODES

Taking pictures is so yesterday though, isn't it? Smartphones are loaded with different modes and Samsung is obviously no stranger to some really great ones.

Think of modes like different lenses. You have your basic camera lens, but then you can also have a lens for fisheye and close up. If you look at the bottom of your camera app, you can slide left and right to get to the different modes.

There are three main ones in the app: photos (which I covered above), videos, and Single Take.

If you've had a smartphone before, then video will probably be familiar to you, but Single Take will probably be new.

Quickly, the video mode has similar features to photo mode. Starting at the bottom, you can pick the kind of video you are taking—three leaves will pull the zoom back and give a wider shot, and one leaf will pull it in and give a closer one.

Up on top, the menu is largely the same as the photo one.

Just like the other modes, pinching in and out will let you zoom in and out.

Single Take is a pretty cool mode. When you press it, it starts recording a 15 second clip. There are no filters or ratios you can change here. It's stripped down.

The beauty of this mode is what it's doing is using a computer to pick the best photo from the video. When the fifteen seconds are up, it will start populating them.

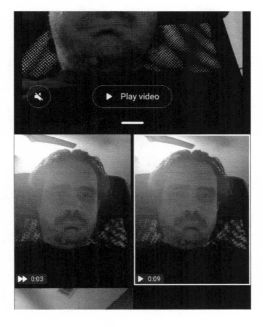

If you click the More option on the slider, you'll see that there are actually several more photography modes on the phone. Twelve more modes to be exact.

AR Doodle used to be a feature in video recording, but it's now been moved to its own camera mode. The mode let's draw things as you record.

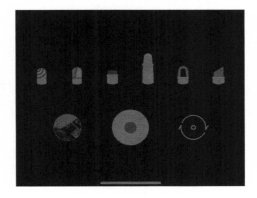

If you thought the Photo mode was a little lacking in options and settings, wait until you see the Pro mode!

You can adjust things like ISO, auto focus and more.

There's also a Pro Video mode with a similar feature set.

Panorama lets you create a panoramic photo; it's great for landscape and cityscape shots.

Food changes settings to give the most ideal focus and effects to take food photos.

Night mode will help you get great shots in low lighting.

Super Slow-Mo, Slow motion and Hyperlapse let you capture either slow motion videos or time-lapse videos.

The final mode is called Director's View, and it's pretty awesome! It lets you record video with both the front and back facing camera at the same time. It's perfect for capturing people's reaction, doing tours, and more. When you use it, you'll see the main screen, then the other camera in the lower left corner.

Tap the arrow above Director's View to toggle between the camera you are using. Just tap the preview to switch.

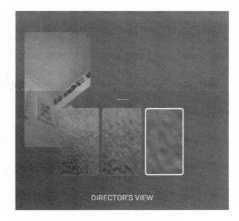

SCREEN ENHANCEMENTS ON THE Z FOLD

With so many cameras on the Z Fold, you'll want to make sure you are taking advantage of all the extra things it does.

With such a large screen, you don't really need to see a preview covering the entire window. If you go to the upper left corner, and tap the scare icon with the columns, then it will split the window in half.

The left column will show a preview of the photos you have taken, and let you scroll through them as you take the photo.

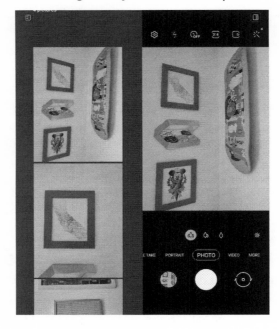

You can also do something similar by folding your phone upward. In the bottom half, you can now swipe over the picture to see the next one in the library.

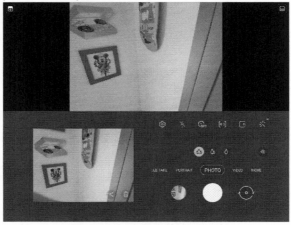

TAKING SELFIES

Of course, the main attraction of the Z Fold is YOU! With so many cameras, you can basically take a selfie no matter how you are holding the phone!

But you don't want to.

The front facing camera on the largest screen is behind the screen itself; it's a decent camera, but not as good as the one on the back of the phone. And the camera on the front of the camera is also subpar compared to the camera on the back. So what do you do? You use that camera for a selfie!

In the upper right corner of the camera is an icon that has a square box with one column. Tap that.

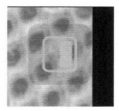

Now turn your phone around. You can use the front screen to preview the photo, but it's actually using the back cameras (which are now to the left of your front preview screen) to take photos! Pretty cool, huh!

EDITING PHOTOS

Once you take a photo, you can begin fine tuning it to really make it sparkle. You can access editing by opening the photo you want to make edits to. This is done by either opening it from the camera app by clicking on the photo preview (next to the shutter);

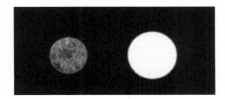

Or by opening the Photo app.

Later in this chapter, I'll write a bit more about how photos are organized, and how you can change things around. For now, we are just talking about editing a photo, so for the purpose of this section, tap on any photo to edit it.

When you open a photo, the options you see will vary depending on what kind of photo you open.

The below example is a Live Focus photo.

As the name suggest, the background is blurred. There's also an option here: Change background effect. This technically isn't editing a photo—when you edit a photo, you go into a different app.

When you tap change the background, you'll have four options. With each option, you can change the intensity of the blur with the slider.

The main blur is simply called "blur"; the next is a spin blur.

The third is a zoom blur.

The last type of blur is color point, which makes the object color and the background black and white.

If you make any changes here, always make sure and tap Apply to save it.

Single Take photos also works a little different when it comes to editing because you have to select which photo you want to edit.

Regardless of the type of photo, there's going to be several options that are the same. Starting on the top, that little play icon will wirelessly show your photo on another device (like a compatible TV).

Next to the play icon is an icon that looks kind of like an eye. That will digitally scan your photo and try and identify what the photo is. In the below example, it finds a flower and gives a link to see more. This feature works pretty good, but isn't always perfect.

Next to the eye icon is an option icon. This will let you set a photo as wallpaper, print it, etc. If you tap Details, it will also let you see when the photo was taken, it's resolution, and any tags that have been assigned to it.

On the bottom of any photo is four additional options. The heard icon favorites the photo, the pencil lets you edit it (more on that in a second), the three dots lets you share it, and the trash lets you delete it.

Tap the pencil icon and let's see how to edit a photo next. Regardless of the photo, you'll see the same options on the bottom.

The first option is to crop the photo. To crop, drag the little white corners.

Next is the filter option. The slider lets you select the type of filter, and below that is a slider to adjust the intensity of the filter.

Brightness is the next icon. Each icon here adjust a different setting (such as the contrast of the photo.

The sticker icon will launch Bitmoji (I'll discuss this later in the chapter), but what this does is let you put stickers on top of your photo.

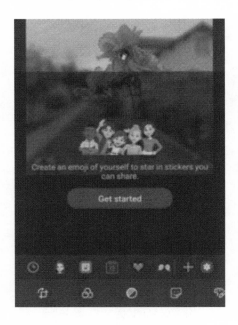

The paintbrush icon lets you draw on top of your photo.

And the text icon lets you write on top of your photo.

If you don't want to spend time editing your photo—you just want it to magically look better with no effort, there's an option up in the upper left corner that will do that for you—it crops, rotates, and adds a filter to it. Depending on how well you took the shot, you may not see much difference.

In the upper right corner is an options menu with even more choices for editing your picture..

The first is Spot Color. Using the little pickers, you can remove a color from the photo to make the subject stand out. To save any changes here, make sure and tap the checkmark; to cancel changes, tap the X.

Style applies filters that give the photo more of an artistic pop—if you want your photo to look like a painting, for example. The slider below it will adjust the intensity.

The advanced option will let you do color corrections.

If you took a photo at the highest resolution and are having difficulty sharing it, you can use the Resize image option to make it smaller.

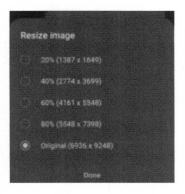

Once you are finished doing edits, make sure and tap Save.

EDITING VIDEOS

Editing a video shares a lot of common features to photos, so make sure and read that section first, as I will not repeat features already referenced above.

To get started open the video that you want to edit, then tap to play it. In the play window, there's going to be a couple of things you should note.

Over on the upper left side you'll see the icon below. This lets you capture a photo from the video. You can do it with any resolution, but you'll find the best photos will come from an 8K video.

Over on the upper right side, is a GIF button. This will let you create a GIF from your video.

You'll notice the video has the same options at the bottom of it (assuming you haven't played it). To edit it, just tap on that pencil.

The first option you'll see is the crop the video. To crop just drag in or out the white bars before and after the video clip.

Next is the color filter, which works almost identically to the photo filter.

The text icon comes after this and lets you write on top of the photo.

The emoji sticker insert is after this.

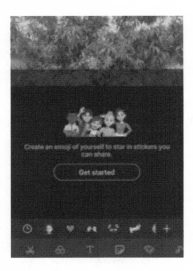

And the paintbrush is second to last.

The last icon is for adding sound. You can add music or anything else you want. You can also use the slider under Video sound to make the videos original sound softer (or nonexistent)—so, for example, you could remove all sound from a family dinner, and replace it with music.

Up on top, there's one option: resolution. If you've recorded in 8K and it's too large, you can use this option to make it smaller.

ORGANIZING YOUR PHOTOS AND VIDEOS

The great thing about mobile photos is you always have a camera ready to capture memorable events; the bad thing about mobile photos is you always have a camera ready to capture events, and you'll find you have hundreds and hundreds of photos very quickly.

Fortunately, Samsung makes it very simple to organize your photos so you can find what you are looking for.

Let's open up the Gallery app and see how to get things organized.

Pixel keeps things pretty simple by having only four options on the bottom of your screen.

There's four additional options up on top.

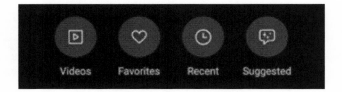

In the upper right corner, there's three dots, which is the photo option menu; that menu is there no matter where you are in the Gallery app.

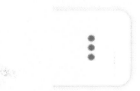

When you tap that menu, you'll get several more options. From this menu you can share an album, create a GIF / collage / Slideshow of the album, or edit the photos / videos in it.

If there's something you are trying to find, tap on the magnifying glass. You can search by what it is (a Live Focus, video, etc), you can search for tags, you can type an expression (happy photos, for example).

When you tap on Albums, you'll see your albums (Samsung will automatically create some for you), and you can tap on options to create a new album.

Stories lets you capture all your life adventures; you can create a new Story the same way you created an album.

The last option is sharing your photos. To get started, tap the red button

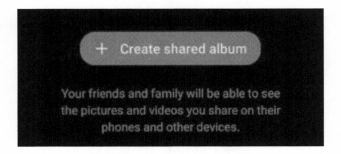

Next, type in a person's phone number or Samsung ID.

Once you have your shared album created, you can tap the + icon to add photos to it.

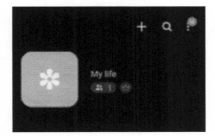

You don't have to add all the photos at once. You can continue to add them over time.

BITMOJI

Bitmoji is the Samsung equivalent of Memoji on the iPhone; it basically lets you create an avatar of yourself that you can use in photos and text messages.

To get started, go to the Camera app, then select More, and finally tap AR Zone.

Next, tap the AR Emoji Camera option.

Before you can have phone, you'll need to take a picture of yourself. Make sure and be in an area with good lighting for the best results.

Once you take the photo, select the gender icon. They are as follows: adult male, adult female, male child, female child. Once you make your select, you'll need wait a few seconds for it to analyze the photo.

Next you can start using the options to change the way you look and what your avatar is wearing.

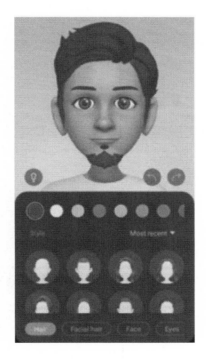

You will now be able to use your AR Camera to take photos with your avatars head replacing others peoples head!

You can also slide over and select other pre-made avatars. My favorite is the Disney one.

On the bottom of the camera is a slider to select the different AR Camera modes. Mirror, for example will put your Avatar in the frame of the photo.

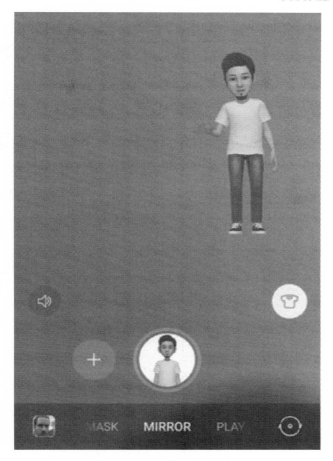

[8]

ADVANCED TOPICS

If you want to take total control of your Samsung, then you need to know where the system settings are and what can and can't be changed there.

First, the easy part: the system settings are located with the rest of your apps. Swipe up and scroll down to "Settings."

This opens all the settings available:

- Connections
- Sounds and vibrations
- Notifications
- Display
- Wallpaper
- Themes
- Home screen
- Lock screen
- Biometrics and security
- Privacy
- Location
- Accounts and backup
- Google
- Advanced features
- Digital Wellbeing and parental controls
- General Management

- Apps
- Battery and Device Management
- Accessibility
- Software update
- Tips and help
- About phone

I'll cover what each setting does in this chapter. There's a lot of settings! Need to find something quickly? Use the magnifying glass up top. Before looking at the settings, however, tap the avatar of the person in the upper right corner. That's going to let you add in personal information.

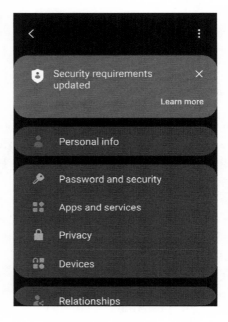

CONNECTIONS

This setting, like most settings, does exactly what it sounds like: it manages how things connect to the Internet, Bluetooth, and NFC payments (i.e. mobile credit cards).

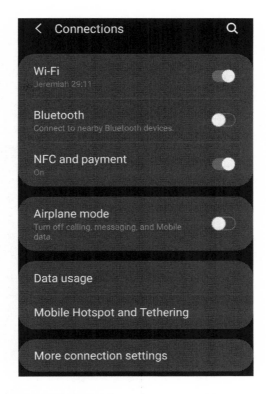

Data usage tells you how much data you've used; tapping on it gives you a deeper overview, so you can see exactly which apps used the data. Why is this important? For most, it probably won't be. I'll give an example of when it helped me: I work on the go a lot; I use the wireless on my phone to connect my laptop (which is called tethering); my MacBook was set to back up to the cloud, and little did I know it was doing this while connecting to my phone...20GB later, I was able to pinpoint what happened by looking at the data.

Below this is Hotspot and tethering. This is when you use your phone's data to connect other devices; you can use your phone's data plan, for example, to use the Internet on your iPad. Some carriers charge extra for this—mine (AT&T) includes it in the plan. To use it, tap the setting and turn it on, then name your network and password. From your other device, you find the network you set up, and connect.

Airplane mode is next. This setting turns off all wireless activity with a switch. So if you're flying and they tell you to turn everything wireless off, you can do it with a switch.

Finally, More connection settings is for doing some wireless connecting on a private network. This is not something a beginning user would need to do, and I'm not going to cover it, as the point of this book is to keep it ridiculously simple. You can also set up wireless printing and wireless emergency alerts here.

SOUNDS AND VIBRATIONS

There's a volume button on the side of your phone, so why would you need to open up a setting for it?! This setting lets you get more specific about your volume.

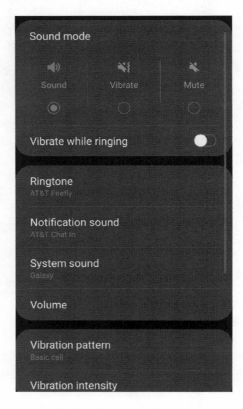

For example, you may want your alarm to ring super loud in the morning, but you want your music to play very low.

You can also use these settings to adjust the intensity of vibrations.

NOTIFICATIONS

Notifications are those pop-ups that give you alerts—like new text messages or emails. In the notification setting you can turn them off for some apps while leaving them on for others. You can also enable Do not disturb mode, which will silence all notifications.

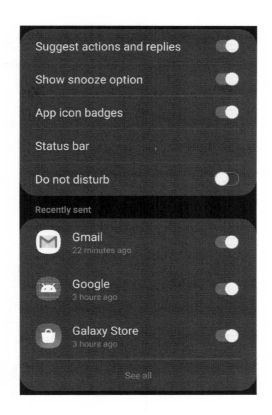

DISPLAY

As with many of the settings, almost all the main features of the Display setting can be changed outside of the app (in the notifications drop-down, for example).

This is where you'll be able to toggle on dark mode, adjust the brightness, turn on adaptive brightness, adjust the refresh rate, and toggle blue light on and off.

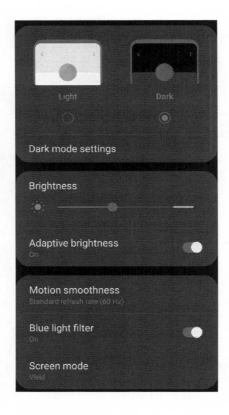

WALLPAPER / THEMES

I'm bundling these two settings together because we've talked about each of them in the section on changing your theme and wallpaper. There are no extra settings here.

HOME SCREEN

This is where you adjust your grid layout (how icons are organized and hide various apps.

LOCK SCREEN

When your phone is on standby and you lift it up: that's your lock screen. It's the screen you see before you unlock it and get to your Home screen.

The settings here change what shows up there; you can also adjust your lock setting—if, for example, you have a Face ID and want to change it to a pin ID.

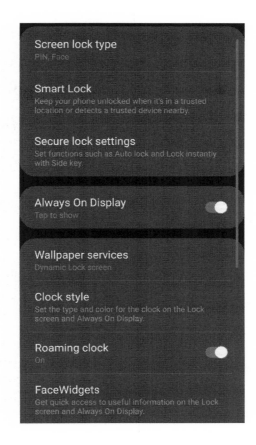

BIOMETRICS AND SECURITY

If you want to add a fingerprint or an additional person to Face ID, you can do so in this menu. You can also update your own—if you didn't do it with glasses, for example, then go here to redo it. You can also toggle on Find My Mobile, which lets you trace where your phone is if you've misplaced it or left it behind.

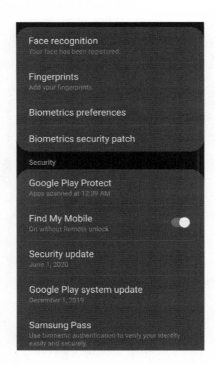

PRIVACY

Like Location Control (covered below), Privacy settings got a big upgrade in Android 10. It's so big, it now fills an entire section in the settings.

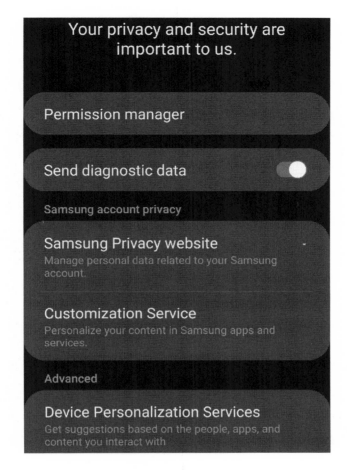

The biggest upgrade is the ability to customize what apps see what; it's no longer all or nothing. You can refine exactly how much or how little each app can see.

Tap on Permissions as one example of what you can control.

LOCATION

In the past, Location Control was an all or nothing feature—you'd decide if an app could see you all the time or none of the time. That's nice for privacy, but not nice for when you actually need someone to know your location—like when you are getting picked up by a ride app like Lyft. The new Android OS adds a new option for while you are using the app. So, for example, a ride app can only see your location while you are using the app; once the ride is over, they can no longer see what you are doing.

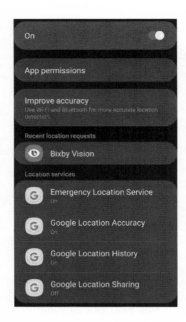

ACCOUNTS & BACKUP

If you have more than one Google account, you can tap on this to add it. If you want to remove your current account, tap on it and tap Remove—remember, however, you can have more than one account. Don't remove it just so you can add another.

You can also come here to back up your phone. It's good to do it once a month or so, but you definitely want to do it before switching to a new device.

GOOGLE

Google is where you will go to manage any Google device connected with your phone. If you are using a Google watch, for example, or a Chromecast.

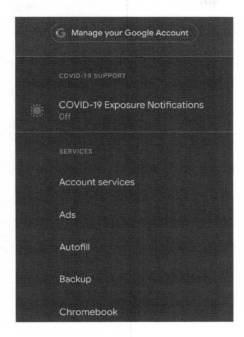

ADVANCED FEATURES

Most the features in Advanced Features are exactly what they sound: Advanced. They're features that novice users will likely never use. Things like screenshot recording features and reducing animations.

There's one important one here. One I recommend everyone use: Side key.

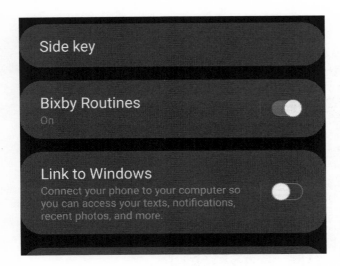

Side key is that button below the volume. Right now, if you hold it down, it goes to Bixby. Bixby isn't Samsung's most popular feature. Some people like it—many don't. If you want to change that button to power down your phone instead, then click that.

When you double tap the button, it launches the camera. You can update that too.

DIGITAL WELLBEING AND PARENTAL CONTROLS

Digital Wellbeing is my least favorite feature on the Samsung phone; now when my wife says, "You spend too much time on your phone"—she can actually prove it! The purpose of the setting is to help you manage your time more. It lets you know you're spending 12 hours a day updating your social media with memes of cats, and "hopefully" make you feel like perhaps you shouldn't do that.

If you have kids using your phone, this is where you can also set up parental controls.

BATTERY AND DEVICE CARE

Samsung tries to make it simple to take care of your phone. With one click (the blue Optimize now), you can have your phone scanned and any problematic apps will be closed.

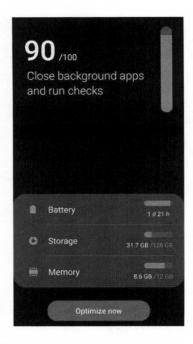

You can also tap on any of the three sections: Battery, Storage, and Memory.

The battery setting is more about analytics than settings you can change. There are some settings here you can edit—you can put your phone in battery saving mode, for example. This setting is more useful if your battery is draining too quickly; it helps you troubleshoot what's going on so you can get more life from your phone.

When you first get your phone, storage won't be a big issue, but once you start taking photos (which are larger than you think) and installing apps, it's going to go very quickly.

The storage setting helps you manage this. It shows you what's taking up storage, so you can decide if you want to delete things. Just tap on any of the subsections and follow the instructions for what to do to save space.

APPS

Every app you download has different settings and permissions. A map app, for example, needs your permission to know your location. You can turn these permissions on and off here. Does it really matter? App makers can't abuse it, right? Sort of. Here's an example: a few months ago, a popular ride-sharing app made headlines because it wanted to know where passengers were after they left the ride, so they could promote different restaurants and stores and make even more money. Many felt this was both greedy and an invasion of privacy; if you are of the latter stance, then you could go in here and stop sharing your location.

How? Just tap Advanced then look at all the permissions you are giving away. Go to the permission you are concerned with and toggle the app from on to off.

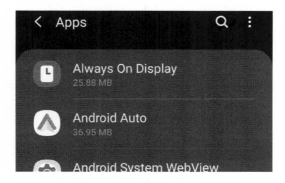

GENERAL MANAGEMENT

General management is where you go to change the language and date / time; the most important thing here, however, is Reset. This is where you can do a complete factory reset of your phone.

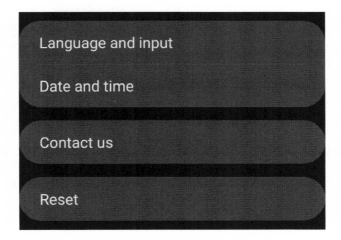

SOFTWARE UPDATE

This is where you will find general information about your phone, such as the OS you are running, the kind of phone you have, IP address, etc. It's more of an FYI, but there are a few settings here that you can change.

TIPS & SUPPORT

This isn't really a setting. It's just tips and support. You can also talk with support here.

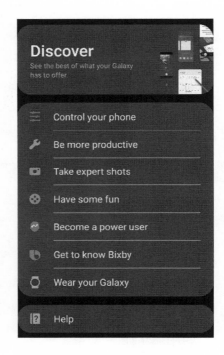

ABOUT PHONE

This is where you will find general information about your phone. Such as the OS you are running, the kind of phone you have, IP address, etc. It's more of an FYI, but there are a few settings here that you can change.

Status

View the SIM card status, IMEI, and other information.

Legal information

Software information

View the currently installed Android version, baseband version, kernel version, build number, and more.

Battery information

View your phone's battery status, remaining power, and other information.

[9]
ADD-ONS

PROJECT FI?

In 2015, Google launched something they called Project Fi. It's their vision of what a cell phone network is supposed to be. A shared plan with a healthy amount of data. You pay for what you need—not what the provider tells you. It's sort of a hybrid of using data and using wi-fi to get you good speeds for a price that's quite a bit cheaper than others.

How much cheaper? It depends, but my guess is cheaper than what you are paying.

As of this writing, it starts at $20. That gets you unlimited minutes and text. But no data. Let's say you are a very light data user and only needed 1GB. It would cost you a total of $30—taxes and fees included. If you are a data hog and stream everything you can 24/7, then you would want the top plan, 20 GB. That would cost you $80. Total. What if you go over 20GB? Same price! Your speed is slowed—that's the catch. It's guaranteed fast until 20GB, however. According to Google, less than 1% of all people use more than 15GB...so chances are, you'll be fine.

What about families? For a family of six, the most you would pay is $275—that's, again, sharing 20GB. You can see a calculator at https://fi.google.com/about/plan/.

S PEN

The S Pen helps you be even more productive on the Z Fold5, but there are a few things you should no: one, it's an optional device (meaning you have to pay extra for it); two, the S Pen you might already own probably won't work on it. You need a fold edition S Pen.

USING THE S PEN

Air Command is the most commonly used feature of the S Pen; Air command is a menu that shows all the features available. To open it, hover the S Pen over the screen and press the S Pen button near the tip.

Available Air Command features are as follows:

- Create Note
- View all notes
- Smart select
- Screen write
- Live messages
- AR Doodle
- Translate
- PENUP
- Bixby Vision
- Magnify
- Glance
- Coloring
- Write on Calendar
- Add Shortcut

While pressing and holding the S Pen button, you can drag the S Pen over text or other items to select them (you can also copy and paste the selected items).

The pen is very simple, yet powerful to use. Tap the screen to activate it. When it's activated, you'll see a small icon on your screen with controls (known as the Air Command).

When you tap that icon, you'll see all kinds of shortcuts available

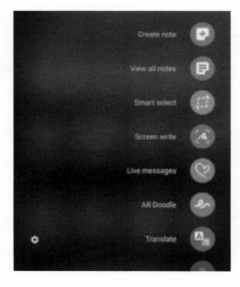

You can also tap the config button to show an expanded list of S Pen settings. This includes shortcut actions.

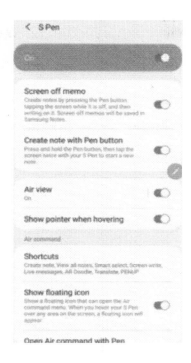

INDEX

ABOUT THE AUTHOR

Scott La Counte is a librarian and writer. His first book, *Queit, Please: Dispatches from a Public Librarian* (Da Capo 2008) was the editor's choice for the Chicago Tribune and a Discovery title for the Los Angeles Times; in 2011, he published the YA book The N00b Warriors, which became a #1 Amazon bestseller; his most recent book is *#OrganicJesus: Finding Your Way to an Unprocessed, GMO-Free Christianity* (Kregel 2016).

He has written dozens of best-selling how-to guides on tech products.

You can connect with him at ScottDouglas.org.

Made in the USA
Las Vegas, NV
27 August 2023

76718572R00106